BOEING 727
SCRAPBOOK

by Len and Terry Morgan

Book design by Richard Groh

AERO PUBLISHERS, INC.
329 West Aviation Road, Fallbrook, California 92028

Library of Congress No. 78-72164

ISBN 0-8168-8349-1 Paper
ISBN 0-8168-8344-0 Hardbound

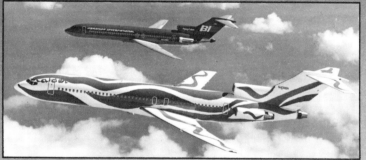

Braniff International Airways commissioned one of the nation's most imaginative artists and creator of the "mobile" art form, Alexander Calder, to render an unusual salute during the American Revolution Bicentennial celebration. For his canvas, Calder selected the 727, mainstay of the line's domestic fleet. Working in his studios in Connecticut and France, the artist experimented with several large models of the aircraft. The final design was scaled up and applied to a full size aircraft at Dallas under his personal supervision. Symbolic of the waving American flag and dubbed, "Flying Colors of the United States," the plane carries the artist's signature above the main cabin door. The company name appears nowhere on the aircraft.

CONTENTS

"6A? All right, Sir."

LaGuardia, late Friday afternoon, the busiest hour of the busiest day. You pick up a final edition of the Daily News, walk across the high-ceilinged lobby past the spotlit bust of Fiorello, past the Hoffritz windows filled with knives, around the corner and down the ramp leading to Gates 11 through 21. You want 18. In your pocket is a ticket to ride Braniff 5 to the Dallas — Ft. Worth Airport.

Work done in Manhattan, a businessman homeward bound for the weekend, you are typical of the actors on this stage. You have played the scene a dozen or fifty or two hundred times before as have many of the strangers in the building who make for their own planes. Most walk, a few hurry and one runs down the hallway. Your watch reads 4:45 so no need to rush. Braniff 5 leaves at 5:00, appropriately. In an hour all of you will be in flight miles from this place and different planes will wait at the gates as new actors walk the stage toward them.

"Hot coffee?"

You clear security and go to the counter, hand over the ticket and pick a seat. The agent removes the "6A" gummed label from the large cabin floor plan, sticks it on the envelope and wishes you a pleasant trip. Outside stands the machine with which the airline proposes to meet its end of the bargain and you recognize it immediately as a Boeing 727. The high T-shaped tail, engines in back and a lean, fast look make the 727 easy to recognize — not like the 707 and DC-8 which look like twin sisters, no matter if they are products of rival builders. You've read somewhere that more than 1,400 727s have been built, some sort of record for airliners. There are plenty of them at LaGuardia, certainly — Eastern, TWA, American, Delta, United and National 727s are lined up out there for take-off.

Down the passageway and into Flight 5, its heavy cabin door swung back to the left, looking stout enough to protect a safe. A stewardess flashes a quick plastic smile and advises that your seat is in the forward cabin, which you already knew. You wonder again if every stewardess on every airline automatically treats every fare as if he had never flown before. You take your seat and she's there, offering to take your coat and fix coffee or a drink before departure. You decide that first impressions are not always lasting. In the hushed interior there are the muted sounds of recorded music, a distant conversation, rustling newspapers. Somewhere beneath the floor a baggage bin door slams closed. The seat is comfortable and

will become more so when it may be tilted after takeoff. The leg room is ample.

No matter how casually you have come to play the role of air traveler or how slight your interest in matters aeronautical, you are at this moment, at least to some degree, "airminded." After all, you are entrusting yourself to this machine, its crew and an unseen force of ground experts along the route from New York to Texas who will render assistance in the complex business about to begin. As a rider, you are powerless to influence any aspect of the process. No thinking individual, however seasoned, becomes so blasé about flying as to — well, stop thinking about it, and being at least mildly curious about the men and mechanisms involved.

The main cabin door is closed, the engines started and you move toward the runway, the taped dance band replaced by the usual admonition to recheck seat belts and return seat backs and tray tables to their full upright positions. You know it by heart. The girl picks up your half-finished glass, promising a fresh drink when airborne.

Why did they call this the 727? Why don't we name airliners as do the British? They came up with *Comet, Britannia, Vanguard* and *Viscount,* and now there's the *Concorde.* We had the *Electra* and *Constellation,* of course, but ours have been mostly numbers — DC-3, DC-6, DC-10, 404, 440, 880, 707, 737, 747. And 727. Numbers are sexless. They don't stir the imagination or kindle the fires of excitement and adventure. You idly wonder if any other passenger aboard clings to the notion that air travel is still something of an adventure.

Number One for takeoff, you sit at the end of LaGuardia's Runway 31, awaiting release. Then, engine sound increases and you are rolling, slowly to begin with, then faster, then racing along over the rough concrete at Indy 500 velocity. The nose rises and flight begins; an instant later the runway whips back out of sight and you stare at the oily waters of Rikers Island Channel. A turn to the right, straight ahead, climbing rapidly, then one to the left and there it is — Manhattan neatly framed in your window, a glorious view from this level. From 3,000 feet, or are you now 4,000 or 5,000? Why don't they put altimeters where passengers can see them?

Chimes sound and the seat belt light goes out. She keeps her promise, also bringing cheese and crackers after draping the table with white linen embroidered with the airline mono-

gram. Before you notice you don't have them, a knife and napkin arrive. Sharp girl. New York is gone so that must be the New Jersey coast. Too high now to see much anyway. Tilt back another notch. Perfect. Big improvement over the DC-6 days, this. That was a while back! Big steel propellers out there shimmering in the sunshine; pounding along, hour after hour. Lots of vibration and noise. Seems like a hundred years ago.

These jets are the way to go. Faster, less tiring, safer. Stay above the weather; get there on time more often. This one is particularly nice. The Boeing 727. That Boeing outfit builds great planes. If only they built cars. Who was — or is — Boeing, the man?

The dinner cart is rolled down the aisle. Roast beef. Looks good.

Be home in three hours.

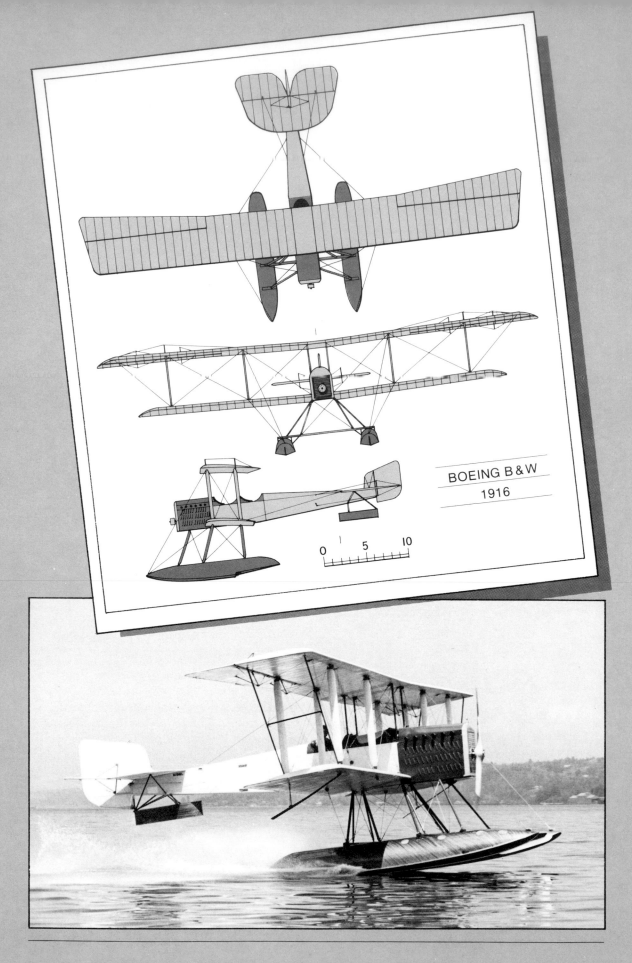

BOEING B&W
1916

0   5   10

William Boeing

Left: Boeing's first airplane was built by carpenters, shipwrights, cabinet makers and seamstresses. Their materials: steel wire, linen, and fine Washington State spruce. The factory: a boathouse on Seattle's Lake Union.

William E. Boeing was born in Detroit in 1881. A Yale graduate, he entered the lumber business at Seattle. At the age of thirty-three he took his first plane ride and became convinced, along with a Naval officer friend named G. Conrad Westervelt, that considerable improvement could be made over existing designs. Their first brainchild, a biplane single-engine floatplane dubbed the "B&W," flew in 1916. When Westervelt was transferred, Boeing reorganized as the Pacific Aero Products Company. Less than a year later and armed with a Navy contract for fifty trainers in his pocket, he set up shop as the Boeing Airplane Company. Here he stands on a float of his C-700, a development of his Model 5. Boeing and one Edward Hubbard put this ship to work in 1919 carrying mail between Seattle and Victoria, B. C. and to ships at sea. A straightforward design powered by a Hall-Scott water-cooled straight-four rated at 100 horsepower, the C-700 clattered along at a mile a minute.

In posed hangar shot (see P-12 pursuits outside), fashionable sextet sample Model 80 luxury and manage to appear suitably blasé about the whole idea of air travel. Billed as the "Pioneer Pullman of the Air," the 80's swivel seats and adjustable reading lamps were unabashed copies of appointments found in a Broadway Limited chair car. What better way to convince the hesitant that air travel had become a perfectly normal and unspectacular experience? And so it was, wind and weather permitting — the breath-taking rush across the grass, the earth dropping away until roads became winding threads and the cars on them creeping ants, the remarkable changing panorama beyond the big windows, the hypnotic drone and vibration of the big radial suspended out there between the glistening wings. And then, almost before you knew it, dropping down with power reduced, the ground rising to meet the wheels, the cabin resuming its original tilt and disappointment that it's over. Truly, it was worth twice the price! "I flew back from Chicago yesterday," was hard to top as an opening gambit in 1930.

Spanking new Model 80, dressed up for airline duty. Shrouds around extended exhaust stack on center engine provided heated air for cabin. The drag rings (engine cowlings) were removed in airline service. The fuselage was formed of welded steel tubing and the wings built of steel spars and dural ribs. Excepting the nose section, the entire airframe was fabric covered. Four hundred gallons of fuel provided a 545-mile range. Fully loaded and gassed, the 80 weighed 15,276 pounds. That weight of jet fuel will keep a 727 in flight two hours and four minutes.

The 80A

Ask the next 727 crewman you see if his plane is the first three-engine airliner built by Boeing. If he says no, he's probably nearing retirement. Or he's a history buff. No is correct.

Boeing's first tri-motor transport was Model 80, conceived, built and flown during 1928 for service on the San Francisco — Chicago run of the company's own airline, Boeing Air Transport. (Federal action six years later was to prohibit aircraft and engine builders from owning airlines with the result that BAT and three other pioneer lines joined in a corporation known to this day as United Air Lines.)

The 80 was a large and handsome biplane of metal airframework covered with fabric. Its reliable Pratt & Whitney "Wasp" radials pulled it along at 115 mph. Twelve passengers rode in unprecedented luxury, their whims catered to by the first stewardess carried as a regular crewmember. She was a registered nurse, which says something about early air travel. After four 80s were completed, the improved 80A was introduced with seats for eighteen. Its P&W "Hornets" were rated at 525 horsepower each (115 more than the "Wasp") and in-

creased cruise by ten miles an hour. Eleven more were delivered.

Reuben Wagner remembers them. "I logged 1,653 hours and 38 minutes in 80s and 80As on the Omaha — Chicago and Omaha — Cheyenne routes between April, 1930, and September, 1933, when they were phased out in favor of the new Boeing 247," he recently recalled. "The 80A was a strong, rugged airplane and a pleasure to fly even when we had to hedge hop during bad weather or because of strong headwinds. It had two-way radiotelephone equipment and could be landed on any grass field used by the single-engine Boeing 40B and 95. That tri-motor had a fine record. No passengers or crewmembers were ever lost even though there were a couple of bad accidents. Everyone walked away from them. It was one of the most rugged and safest airplanes Boeing ever built. The only complaint I can recall — and it was very minor indeed — was that the windshield would smear from oil thrown back by the center motor."

Not all of the open cockpit drivers took to the 80's enclosed working quarters, a few insisting that a proper job could only be performed outdoors in helmet, goggles and heavy leather coat. One ship was in fact redesigned as the 80B with exposed and elevated seats which allowed pilot and copilot to see back over the top wing. Anyone who has occupied an open cockpit

The Model 80B

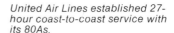
United Air Lines established 27-hour coast-to-coast service with its 80As.

Boeing 80A NC32M drifts slowly down final approach on a warm day (note captain's open window). This improved eighteen-seater grossed out at 17,500 pounds and could struggle up to 14,000 feet, scarcely enough to top some ranges west of Denver. Range — 460 statute miles; touchdown speed — 61 miles an hour. Captain Wagner remembers having to refuel at emergency grass strips when headwinds cut groundspeed to less than that of freight trains. "The copilot had to gas this big airplane with five-gallon cans. When he was through, the pile of empties was as high as the plane." The first airline copilots also loaded bags, collected tickets, passed out box lunches and kept track of flight progress. Weather and the whims of their captains determined the extent to which they actually handled the controls aloft. On some lines, these in-flight assistants paid for their apprenticeships. On others the stipend averaged fifty to a hundred dollars a month. Present day first officers take note.

in mid-winter will understand why the modification lived a short life. The B was rebuilt to 80A configuration at the insistence of the majority.

What a book could be written about Reuben Wagner's flying career! He left Nebraska in 1917 to enlist in the Army Signal Corps, completing military flight training in Texas in 1919. Then he barnstormed through the midwest for four years in a Curtiss Jenny, flying Army equipment on weekends as a Reserve officer. In 1923 he signed on to fly the mail in the DH-4 powered by a 12-cylinder Liberty engine, beginning an airline career lasting until July, 1957, when he completed his last DC-7 schedule.

His logbooks reflect the astounding development of American air transportation from the original mail experiment to acceptance of flying as the best way to get there. They reflect the energy and vision of the man himself and the pilots of his day who saw more on the horizon than trees. A founding member of the Air Line Pilots Association, his gold card presented at retirement bears the number 13. The last trip brought his total flying time to 31,946 hours and nine minutes. What memories of men and planes and places and events the logbook entries must bring to mind.

What stories Captain Reuben Wagner, United Air Lines, Retired, can tell.

A Word About Francis & Amos . . .

Pratt & Whitney. It is often assumed that the title of the Connecticut engine builders includes the names of its founders — a Mr. Pratt and a Mr. Whitney, whomever they may have been. In fact, neither gentleman ever left the ground nor built an aircraft engine, though there is a connection between what they did and the huge organization which bears their names today. Some years ago, Paul Fisher and John Smith provided this explanation:

Mr. Pratt, & Mr. Whitney, the Ampersand

by Paul Fisher and John Smith

One of our men with a proper Yankee feeling for genealogy set out a few days ago to find out what he could about Mr. Francis Pratt and Mr. Amos Whitney, those nineteenth century gentlemen whose names were bequeathed to Pratt & Whitney Aircraft after their own company had established a world-wide reputation in the machine tool, firearm and precision instrument fields. Both Mr. Pratt and Mr. Whitney were fulsomely bearded, favored derby hats and frock coats, and both could talk a blue streak. None of these facts, our man reported, was ever put in cold print. In fact, he found that the reporters and historians of their era were so busy recording the astonishing range of Mr. Pratt's and Mr. Whitney's improvisations in metal that they never got much written on the way the men personally lived and acted. Our man then forsook the libraries, remembering New England mechanics often live long lives, and sure enough, he found a handful of men who not only remembered Mr. Whitney, who lived until 1920 when he was 88 years old, but had worked with Mr. Pratt, too, whose death took place in 1902 when he was 75. Our man spent a couple of pleasant days chatting with the old-timers, and then reported:

Mr. Pratt was six feet, two inches tall, broad-shouldered, a sparing drinker, a ruthless adversary of the metric system, and a great enigma to the shop people. He could design and build anything in metal, but he was almost never seen in the shop and rarely seen in the design room. Not so Mr. Whitney. Mark Twain was one of their customers, but he wasn't one-two-three with Mr. Whitney as a full-blown swearer. The old mechanics contend Mr. Whitney was the most eloquent and loudest curser in the history of the metal-working industry, which of course drops Twain pretty low, since his art in profanity was a comparatively weak blend of the literary and riparian schools. Moreover, they point out, Mr. Whitney was devout, which Twain wasn't particularly, and the devout man, especially one with an Old Testament background, has a swing to his style lacking in the less pious. Mr. Whitney was a pillar in the Universalist Church; a saying used to exist in Hartford that there wasn't an unemployed Universalist in town as long as Mr. Whitney was running the Pratt & Whitney tool shop.

He had no compunction about appearing among his men in his shirt sleeves, but none of them — excepting the Universalists who saw him in church on the Sabbath — ever caught him without his derby on. Like Mr. Pratt, he was a genius with machinery, but Mr. Whitney also had one other gift. He was a wizard at getting drunks out of bed.

Mr. Whitney's Preserve

The shop was Mr. Whitney's preserve. Every morning at exactly 7 o'clock for almost fifty years prior to his death, he drew up at the shop door in a buggy drawn by one of many generations of big chestnut horses, and clambered down. He was around five feet, seven inches tall, big-shouldered, and usually wore a diamond stick-pin and a large gold watch-fob. No one remembers him ever varying the ritual that then followed. He trudged about the room running an intelligent thumb over the machined surfaces of the metal being worked, and the moment his thumb encountered an imperfection, he let out a roar and called down imprecations and called up the culprit. With the scrutiny of the metal completed, he began a second swing around the shop. If a man was missing from his accustomed place, he inquired if he had been sent out on another piece of work or simply was absent, Mr. Whitney took a small black notebook from his pocket and jotted down the man's name. Once his check of the working force had been finished, he returned to his buggy, and drove off to the home of the absent man. There he consulted the man's wife, and if the man was ill, he sent for a doctor, provided money for drugs and food and bolstered the ill man's spirits. If the man was drunk or recovering from a drunk, Mr. Whitney had him out of bed and in the buggy in a matter of minutes and at work shortly thereafter. He was a great believer in the therapeutic value of action to relieve alcoholism. He himself was a teetotaler.

Able craftsmen with a lazy streak sometimes found Mr. Whitney bearing down on them and hauling them off to his shop, although they were unaware that they were on his payroll. His explanation would be honest; the man's wife had come to him and said he wouldn't work and the cupboard was getting bare, and would Mr. Whitney do something about it? He generally would and did.

Mr. Pratt and Mr. Whitney first met in Colt's Pistol Factory, which in the 1840s and 1850s served as a national graduate school for gifted mechanics, just as in the years to come Pratt & Whitney Company itself was to serve similarly. Mr. Pratt's solicitude for accuracy had been with him since his early boyhood; he believed that accuracy to the accepted thirty-second of an inch, considered sound in his apprentice days, was far too inexact for real progress. He believed if precisions to the ten thousandths of an inch and the millionths of an inch could be achieved, then the world of mechanics could be revolutionized. Two years after he came to Colt's from Lowell, Massachusetts, he was made superintendent of the Phoenix Iron Works of Hartford, and not long thereafter Mr. Whitney transferred to Phoenix, too. Mr. Whitney foresaw, if real accuracy could be achieved, the possibility of an age where machinery

would lift the heaviest burdens. Their joint ideal was an accuracy finer than could be seen by the human eye or measured with known instruments, and out of this mutual interest came the nighttime pooling of their labors in a little Hartford back room, beginning in 1860. Although their success in the designing and developing of tools was almost instantaneous, they continued to work at Phoenix (later the Taylor and Fenn Company) until 1865, long after their own shop's reputation was national in scope, a native New England caution they seldom exhibited thereafter.

Mr. Pratt and Mr. Whitney had an immense dissatisfaction with the inch from the beginning. Every craftsman complained that the old saying was true, "Every yardstick is its own measure." So Mr. Pratt and Mr. Whitney established the inch. They engaged William A. Rogers, a professor of astronomy at Harvard College, and George M. Bond, a graduate of Stevens Institute of Technology, to create a comparator for absolutely correct measurements within a limit of one fifty-thousandths of an inch.

Standard Yard Lost in Fire

The standard yard had been destroyed in the great London fire of 1834, and in evolving the historically famous Rodgers-Bond Comparator, Mr. Pratt and Mr. Whitney had four copies made of Bronze No. 1, the standard measure that replaced the destroyed measure. Bronze No. 1 is made of Bailey's metal and measures thirty-eight inches in length, one inch in depth and one inch in width.

The old-timers said they remembered as if it had happened only yesterday that after Mr. Bailey's death, two Englishmen were delegated to carry on with the Bronze, and could our man guess their names? He couldn't. Well, said the old-timers, grinning, maybe it wasn't a good laugh in the mid-twentieth century, but back in the nineteenth century everyone had been pleased when the Reverend Sheepshank and Mr. Ramsbottom were appointed to carry on for Mr. Bailey.

Professor Rogers also succeeded in obtaining a reliable transfer of both the French Meter d'Archives and the American standard of length known as Bronze No. 11, and out of all this research came the Pratt & Whitney Standard Measuring Machine, which today is known throughout the world as the basis for the construction and duplication of recognized standards of length.

With accuracy thus established to the precision they had dreamed, Mr. Pratt and Mr. Whitney were ready for the tide of inventions that followed — sewing machines, typewriters, typesetters, automatic counting and weighing machines, telephones, motor cars, aircraft — the mechanical world that burgeoned with interchangeability.

They had established the precision essential to such close tolerances as interchangeable parts required, and in the generations that followed, their craftsmen built the machine tools to create the new machinery. There was no Pratt & Whitney specialization. They built all varieties of lathes, boring mills, shapers, planers, vertical drills, multiple drills, grinders, screw machines, tapping machines, cam cutting machines, die sinkers, profilers, broaching presses, power hammers, cranes and a wide range of gages, taps, dies and drills. Mr. Pratt was a scrupulous designer and craftsman. He was also an extraordinarily vivid salesman. He began going abroad in the 1870s, and he sold Pratt & Whitney products in every corner of Europe and the Orient; indeed, sales and deliveries were made to Siberia. Our man found that one reporter once had remembered to jot down one of his remarks. Mr. Pratt said that for his company "the world is its field, and therefore, it is only necessary to seek business in a liberal and intelligent way to secure it every time in the open market." Literally millions of machine tools, gages, and other instruments went to every corner of the world bearing the mark, "Pratt & Whitney Co., Hartford, Conn., U.S.A."

Fred Schuster, a veteran of sixty years with Pratt & Whitney, told our man that he used to watch Mr. Pratt in action as a salesman. He said Mr. Pratt would remain seated, opposite his caller, chatting along, until he decided to make a point, and then abruptly, he would raise himself to his awesome height, peer down with his keen dark eyes, "and," said Mr. Schuster, "then speak as though from Olympus." Mr. Schuster thinks Mr. Pratt was one of the deftest men in the world in flabbergasting "those men who pose as authorities." "He'd pretend to be impressed with all the outpourings on technical matters from the fellow," Mr. Schuster said, "and then with one swoop, he'd wipe the fellow away by a display of technical and working knowledge of machinery that was unmatchable. As a designer, he was a wonder — inventive, exacting and absolutely sure."

Anti-Metric Leader

As a leader of the anti-metric society (both that group and those favoring the metric system were powerful and articulate organizations in the late nineteenth century), Mr. Pratt struck hard and often. Nothing infuriated him quite so much as the attempt by the International Society for Standard Measure to impose an edict that one natural basis for standard measures should be the arc of a pendulum in a vacuum at 62 degrees F. at sea level in London, England. The old-timers said Mr. Pratt saw red on that one, and finally got it abolished. It was about that time that Mark Twain was around Pratt & Whitney a good deal, in the interests of the Paige typesetter, whose development cost Twain a pretty penny. The machine proved far too expensive to build, but Pratt & Whitney people recall that its design formed the basis of the Mergenthaler and other typesetting machines used today. Pratt & Whitney made a host of famous firearms — the Lee-Enfield rifle, the Gardner machine gun, which U. S. Grant called "the best arm of the kind he had ever seen," the .37 mm. Hotchkiss gun, and the Springfield rifle. They built the Kidder typewriter in 1900, the ancestor of the present noiseless typewriter.

Discarded Imperfect Work

Mr. Whitney was a rarity in the nineteenth century among metal men in his approach to defective material. When he encountered a forging or casting that was imperfect, he muttered into his beard, and then loudly ordered it tossed aside. His principles of quality and precision attracted skilled men from every corner of the country, and the roster of Pratt & Whitney graduates who rose to fame in the machine tool and allied industries is extraordinary — for instance, Warner, Swasey, Foote, Gleason, Bullard, La Pointe, and Gardner are names known wherever metal is worked, and all of those men were trained at Pratt & Whitney under the direct supervision of Mr. Whitney.

From the outset, our man found, Mr. Pratt and Mr. Whitney abolished the word "and" and substituted the ampersand symbol in their trade name. Neither at Pratt & Whitney Company nor at Pratt & Whitney Aircraft, to be sure, is it wrong legally to spell out the *and*, but precedence and consistency call for the symbol. The precedent now is ninety years old. At the height of the war, a colored man, 94 years old, applied at Pratt & Whitney Aircraft Corporation of Missouri for a job, and

Home of the world's largest producer of gas turbine engines, the Pratt & Whitney plant at Rentschler Field, East Hartford, keeps 33,000 workers busy. Another 10,000 are employed at facilities in Florida and Canada. Some 57,000 engines were completed through 1976, nearly all of them for aircraft use, military buyers taking seventy-five percent of these. The claim is made that P&W-powered service aircraft hold the records for highest altitude performance, highest speed, fastest climb to altitude, longest range of unrefueled flight and highest authorized time between overhauls. Pratt & Whitney is a division of United Technologies (formerly United Aircraft).

when he was told gently that he was a little old for the work, he demanded the right to see either Mr. Pratt or Mr. Whitney. "They're bound to be drier behind the ears than you young whippersnappers," he said hotly, which, of course, was quite true.

"Mr. Pratt, Mr. Whitney and the Ampersand" *originally appeared in Pratt & Whitney Aircraft's house organ, the* Bee Hive, *and is reprinted courtesy of that publication.*

The Man Who Built Engines

The son of an Ohio machine tool company executive, Frederick B. Rentschler graduated from Princeton, then entered the family shops to learn the machinist's trade at first hand. Like many young Americans of his day, he fell in love with the internal combustion engine, and this romance was to have far-reaching effects. During the First World War he served as a Signal Corps officer, inspecting Hispano-Suiza engines built under license in New Jersey. He left the Army convinced that a new approach was needed to the riddle of aircraft power. Planes of the future would require engines much lighter, more powerful and reliable than anything he had seen so far.

In 1919 he helped organize the Wright Aeronautical Corp., became its president and had the company operating in the black after the first year. His team of designers eventually created remarkable products, including the J-5 radial which powered a number of successful planes, among them the *Spirit of St. Louis.* By 1924 Wright had become, in one historian's view, "the outstanding engine company in the country," yet Rentschler was unhappy. The Wright directors did not share his philosophy that profits should be plowed back into research, that development dollars spent now would result in larger profits in five to ten years. In 1924, at age thirty-seven, he resigned and walked out.

Rear Admiral William A. Moffett listened to Rentschler's argument that the air-cooled radial concept promised more power and reliability per pound than anything the water-cooled builders had so far produced or had in mind. Furthermore, added the intent engineer, he could quickly assemble a company to do the job. The admiral, thinking of the two hundred aircraft needed to equip the *Saratoga* and *Lexington,* two carriers about to be launched, was impressed. The Navy was interested, he said, but could not afford a development contract.

Rentschler called on an old family friend, the president of Niles-Bemont-Pond Co., outlined his ideas and pointed out that one N-B-P shop was standing idle in the postwar slump. This location — the Pratt & Whitney division — was where engines could be built. One more thing: he needed $250,000 to get going, and a million more upon receipt of the first order. That these conditions were met within days says all that need be said about the man's reputation and powers of persuasion. The Pratt & Whitney Aircraft Company was in business. Consider the day in which this remarkable deal was made — the

Rentschler (behind crate) and engineering assistants accompanied first production "Wasp" to loading dock on Dec. 17, 1928. Within sixty days, fifteen engines a month were being delivered to the Navy's initial order for 200 engines.

services had precious few dollars budgeted for aircraft and the first airline was yet to be founded. General opinion of flying had been summed up by Rentschler's own father who called it a "damn fool business, mostly for sportsmen."

Even more remarkably, P&W's first engine, dubbed the "Wasp" at the suggestion of Mrs. Rentschler, was assembled and ready for test within eight months. During factory run-in and later tests in Navy aircraft, the "Wasp" exceeded all expectations.

The rest is history.

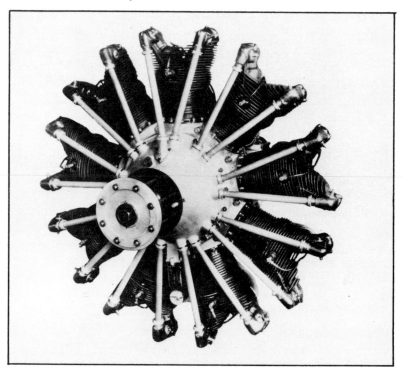

The original P&W "Wasp." Its specifications: bore and stroke — 5.75 inches: displacement — 1,300 cubic inches; compression ratio — 5.25:1; rating — 400 horsepower at 1,900 revolutions per minute; dry weight — 650 pounds. Rear-mounted accessories included dual Scintilla magnetos, Stromberg carburetor, fuel and oil pumps. A starter and generator were optional. The prototype never flew and is preserved today in the Smithsonian collection. It bears between its lower cylinders the same flying eagle trademark affixed to P&W engines to this day. Cost to the Navy — $15,385.92. Production "Wasps" were delivered at $7,730.00 each. In-flight tests were conducted in several Navy types, one being Boeing's Model 69, a shipboard fighter designated the F2B-1. Thus began more than a half century of successful Boeing airframe/Pratt & Whitney powerplant combinations.

JT8D

The P&W JT8D, three of which power every 727 built, was first tested in 1961 since when it has undergone extensive development resulting in nine basic models, some of which are available in three variations. A specific engine is known by its "dash number" — the Dash 1A, Dash 15, Dash 17R and so on. The Dash 1 produces 14,000 pounds of thrust for takeoff, the latest Dash 209 being rated at 18,500. The respective dry weights are 3,155 pounds and 4,180. The engine is ten feet long, about three and a half in diameter and is built largely of steel and titanium. The usual accessories are mounted

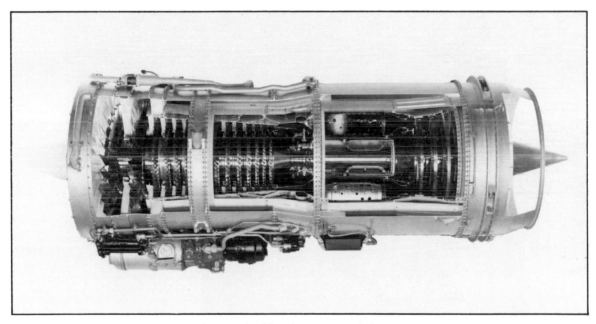

beneath. Numbers 1 and 2 engines of a 727 turn hydraulic pumps; all three turn generators. While P&W improved its engine, Boeing updated its transport. The latest 727-200 series is twenty-one feet longer than the prototype and weighs 67,500 pounds more ready for takeoff. These numbers translate into airline profit dollars. The JT8D also powers the 737, DC-9, some models of the Caravelle and other types. It is said to power more than seventy percent of the world's short /medium range airliners, some 2,300 of them being at work for 135 carriers. Every minute eleven JT8D-powered flights depart, carrying a million passengers a day. Certainly the first one deserves a place alongside the barking little "Wasp" with which it all began.

Twenty-three bladed first stage of forward compressor prior to installation of nose cone. High pressure air is bled through the heavy plumbing seen in this view for use in cabin heating and pressurization and for anti-icing of wings and engine nacelles.

Eight quick-release fasteners are snapped open to expose Number 1 Engine for inspection and maintenance. Now raise the hood of your car and imagine changing the water pump. Airline economics require that malfunctioning components, including entire engines, be replaceable in minimum time. Tedious trouble-shooting and repair can be accomplished later, after the ship is back on schedules with a new part in place. The JT8D is held in position by three bolts. Three experienced mechanics can change it in four hours. If a 727 suffers an engine failure out on the line, it is not out of service until a new engine is brought to it. A specially trained crew ferries it out on two engines and back to the main maintenance base. Minimum fuel is carried to keep weight down and no other riders are permitted aboard. "An airliner is like a mother-in-law," quipped one airline official, "no good on earth." A shop foreman summed it up this way, "There are airplanes and there are flying machines. Airplanes sit in the hangar being fixed while flying machines are out there earning profits."

Fuselage-mounted Number Two sits in tail, not above cabin as is sometimes imagined. Air is drawn through large S-shaped duct with intake at forward base of vertical fin. Ventral stairs leading to rear cabin can be seen through ladder. On the stretched 727, this folding entry must be down during all ground operations for it is possible during fueling and passenger loading to induce sufficient tail-heaviness to make the ship rear back and sit on its tail, DC-3 fashion. It has happened, just as the occasional DC-3 ended up nose down, tail up.

The combustion section with burner cans exposed. Normal starting aboard a 727 is made with air pressure from the auxiliary power unit in the main wheel wells. At twenty-percent of top rotation speed, the captain moves the fuel control lever to "Idle," causing fuel to be injected into the burner cans, two of which are fitted with igniters. The "light off" is almost immediate as ignition spreads to the remaining cans. At forty percent, the starter switch is released, the igniters are deenergized and combustion continues until fuel supply is shut off. The thrust lever (same function as the throttle of a recip) regulates fuel flow and thus power output. During takeoff, landing and flight in precipitation or turbulence, igniters are turned on as a precaution against flame out.

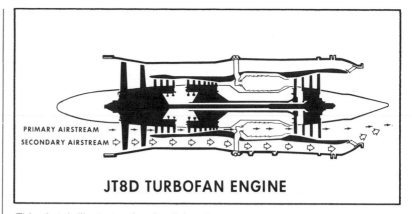

PRIMARY AIRSTREAM

SECONDARY AIRSTREAM

JT8D TURBOFAN ENGINE

This sketch illustrates the simplicity of operation of the JT8D. The forward six-stage (six rows of blades) compressor turns on the same shaft with rear three-stage turbine while outer shaft couples seven-stage compressor with single-stage turbine. The dual assemblies of this "twin-spool" design rotate independently. N_1 (forward compressor and rear turbine) spins at 8,600 revolutions per minute at 100% power, while N2 turns 12,250 rpm. The forward compressor draws in air, feeding a primary supply to the secondary compressor, both of which revolve within a housing of decreasing diameter. The resulting compression reaches 16:1, the high pressure air being forced into the combustion section containing nine "burner cans." Fuel is injected and ignited. The rapidly expanding gases formed have but one way to go — out the tailpipe — which they do with a mighty rush and roar. During their exit they must pass across the turbines, causing them to spin. This in turn rotates the compressors which draw in more air for compression, mixing with fuel and ignition. The first two stages of the forward compressor have meanwhile diverted some air around the engine to mix with hot exhaust gases at the tailpipe. One advantage of such "turbofan" design is quieter operation than that obtained from a "turbojet" which uses all intake air for combustion. The first two stages of the forward compressor — the "fan" — actually work as propellers, making the JT8D a push-and-pull engine. At the peak of reciprocating engine development, the time between overhaul rarely ran above 2,500 hours. In comparison, the TBO time for the JT8D is approaching 17,000 hours. That's nearly two years of continuous running

Bearded Francis and Amos in their high collars, frock coats and derbies would look out of place inspecting the work of JT8D final assembly today, though one can believe they would soon feel at home with these modern machine men. Notice brick floor and labeling of trash barrel, shades of the past.

George Sanborn, Director of Sales, left, looks over
727 proposals with Wellwood Beall, Senior Vice
President. The proposal in front of Beall bears a striking
resemblance to the French Caravelle, a type at one
time considered for production in Boeing's plant.

Return of the Tri-Motor:

Evolution, Design

The 727 design team, from left to right: Ed Pfaffman, hydraulics and flight controls; Fred Maxam, other systems; Joe Sutter, flaps and high lift devices; Jack Steiner, Chief Project Engineer; Reg Watney, structures and Dave Norton, aerodynamics and wind tunnel testing. Maxam felt the 727 should have two engines as suggested by the model in the foreground, and such a design was later built as the 737. During the peak of design work, some 1,500 experts worked under Steiner's direction while recruiters looked for more, at one point "renting" a hundred draftsmen en masse from a Canadian firm.

With sales and orders now over 1,500, the 727 has become the most widely used civil transport in air history. Since its introduction into service in 1964, it has been enthusiastically acclaimed by airmen, passengers, technicians, airline leaders and federal officials. It is exactly the right combination for its time and as close to being "the DC-3 of the jet age" as any turbine airliner is likely to become.

Such success stories do not write themselves. Strangely enough, the 727 project was nearly shelved before it got off the drawing boards. When Boeing engineer Jack Steiner was assigned to explore the idea of building a short/medium range airliner, there was much head-shaking in Seattle. The 707 gamble was only just beginning to pay off and there was fear of rocking the boat. However, after extensive discussions with Eastern, United, TWA and American, Steiner's staff was convinced of the need for a medium size, high performance airline aircraft. The following goals were established:

The secret of the 727's short runway abilities lies in large degree in its sophisticated high-lift flap system. Here engineers (l. to r.) Gerry Bowes, Chuck Kolesar and Dave Norton pose with wind tunnel model. Norton, who reported to Joe Sutter, worked to streamline external parts for smoother air flow.

Scale 727 models underwent 5,500 hours of wind tunnel testing, the highest time ever spent on a new Boeing design.

The new airliner must:

1 — operate profitably from short runways and over short routes,

2 — be quiet enough for acceptance at such close-in airports as LaGuardia,

3 — fly at competitive speeds on short and medium distance runs,

4 — be capable of takeoff from high elevation airfields on hot, windless days,

5 — require a minimum of ground support equipment and personnel,

6 — be easy to fly,

7 — provide a smooth, quiet ride,

8 — have a fuel supply sufficient for bad weather operations,

9 — be able to operate into airports equipped with minimum navigational aids,

10 — be capable of growth.

United's W. A. Patterson placed the initial order — twenty firm and twenty on option. Eastern's Malcolm MacIntyre ordered forty. With eighty orders in hand, a decision had to be made. The amazing story of what transpired between 1956, when Steiner began his studies, and late 1960, when United and Eastern initialed intents to buy, is told in Harold Mansfield's *Billion Dollar Battle,* a fascinating account.

There was understandable apprehension in the Boeing plant the day the word came down from President Bill Allen's office: build the 727.

Work Order 69591 was signed on May 31, 1960, requiring "Engineering to commence production design on the 727 airplane on June 10." The long months of studies, cost analysis, airline conferences and computer calculations resulted in that one piece of paper. It was time to start building. Engineer Ed Pfaffman and his flight controls team were given two million dollars to build this "iron bird," a full size model of the 727's proposed flight control system occupying 130 feet of hangar floor space. It featured computerized "feel," allowing designers to measure control wheel and rudder pedal loads at various flight speeds and test components before installation in the aircraft itself.

Joe Sutter, Chief of the Technical Staff, reflects on the work required to perfect the complex flap system. He had worked previously with Jack Steiner during development of Model 377, the famous Stratocruiser of piston days.

Boeing's Joe Davis (l.) and James Boynton inspect the prototype 727's unique wing flaps, shown here in the "Flaps 15" position used for most takeoffs. During high speed cruising, all flaps are retracted, giving the wing a thin, knife-like shape. Extension of leading and trailing edge flaps at slow approach speeds converts the wing to a high lift, low speed contour which enables pilots to operate from short runways with profitable loads. Twenty-six separate panels are positioned in automatic sequence through operation of a single cockpit lever. Here's the order of events in a typical approach to land:

Your 727 flight has descended from its cruising level to 3,000 feet and is slowing with thrust levers in idle position, still in "clean" configuration (gear and flaps up). Ten miles from the runway, airspeed is down to 200 knots (230 mph), and the pilot at the controls calls for, "Flaps 2." His assistant moves the flap lever to the first slot, causing the trailing edge flaps to move back and down two degrees and two leading edge devices on each wing to fold down and forward. A green light illuminates when the "LEDs" are extended. As speed slows further, the pilot calls, "Flaps 5."

The lever is positioned, trailing edge flaps move to five degrees and the remainder of the LEDs fold out, this again being confirmed by a green light. Moving the flap handle to "15" extends trailing edge flaps furthur. Speed is now stabilized at 150 knots.

About five miles from the runway, the landing gear is extended and the flaps dropped to "25" then "30", the normal landing configuration. (Forty degrees is available in the 727-100 but rarely used). Flap travel past "5" is restricted to the trailing edge panels.

The process is reversed during departure, with flaps being retracted "on schedule" (as speed increases) and as the green light verifies that the LEDs have properly stowed themselves for fast flight.

Extension of the flaps reactivates the outboard ailerons, these being locked in trail during high speed, flaps up flight. In addition, two heavy duty electric fans are switched on to maintain air flow through the air conditioning system and hydraulic input to the rudders shifts to high power, giving the pilot greater advantage during low speed maneuvering.

The entire leading edge of the wing can be warmed during icing conditions with air bled from engine compressors. The long row of oval plates provide access to the wing fuel cell. The small tab inserted in the aileron provides for lateral trimming.

The 707 prototype, the "Dash Eighty," was put to work flight testing the rear engine location and unique wing flap system proposed for the 727. The curved tailpipe fitted to the JT8 served to divert hot gases around the horizontal stabilizer and was not used on the 727. An S-shaped duct is however installed ahead of the 727's center engine to route intake air from the scoop above the fuselage. Considerable work was required to obtain a smooth flow through this duct, small vanes called vortex generators being fitted inside to burble the air for proper engine ingestion.

The chances of having to shut down a JT8 in flight are one in 1,600; the odds against dual powerplant failures are said to be 7,700,000 to one. In order to receive federal certification as an airliner, designers must demonstrate in actual flight tests that their product can suffer complete failure of one engine at the most critical moment of departure — the instant the nose is lifted for takeoff — and climb out of the field to circle back for a normal landing. These demonstrations must of course be conducted with the aircraft fully loaded. Obviously, a four-engine aircraft must continue climb with 75% of normal takeoff power, a 727 with two-thirds of its normal thrust and a two-engine 737 with but half of its power remaining, which explains why twin-engine airliners are more sprightly on takeoff than three- and four-engine types. Interestingly, the first 727 developed exactly the same total takeoff thrust as the original, considerably heavier, 707.

Roll-out of the prototype. Unusual view from hangar roof shows fuel dump nozzles on wing trailing edges near tips, outboard ailerons used in low speed maneuvering and small inboard ailerons installed between trailing edge flap sections. Ground and flight spoiler panels lie flush in upper wing surfaces just forward of ailerons and flaps. Two-piece horizontal elevator is hydraulically-boosted by two independent pressure systems, either of which can provide full control. The forward horizontal stabilizer is raised and lowered by an electrically-powered jackscrew to provide trimming for "hands off" flight under all combinations of load and speed. The small stub wings which attach engines to fuselage house wiring and plumbing. Excessive temperature in these areas is reported by warning lights on the flight engineer's panel. Wing sweep is 35° at the fuselage, 32° for the outboard sections.

First Flight

Smiling Jack Steiner shakes hand of test pilot Lew Wallick as copilot Dix Loesch (on Steiner's left) and flight engineer Marvin Shulenberger look on. Wallick told Steiner, "It's an excellent airplane. The performance exceeded all expectations and her response to control was instantaneous and effortless. Pilots are really going to like this one."
— And pilots do.

It was February 9, 1963, at Renton, Washington. The time had come. The airmen who were on hand, not to learn *if* the 727 would fly, but *how* it flew were R. L. "Dix" Loesch, Jr., Chief of Flight Test, Lew Wallick, Jr., Test Pilot, and Flight Engineer Marvin Shulenberger. The weather was unseasonably clear. The wind was from the north — a requirement as flight testing is restricted to north departures over Lake Washington, rather than south over built-up areas.

Loesch served as copilot on the first hop, assigning Wallick to occupy the left seat. Here's how Wallick remembers that day:

"The first flight was most enjoyable for me because I had been working closely with the engineering staff. After all the long meetings, discussions and simulations, I was anxious to see how close the airplane was to predictions.

"The sun has always shone on the 727. The day of the first flight was beautifully clear and the wind was straight down the runway. The takeoff was routine until shortly after lift-off when the Number 2 engine surged. We reduced thrust on it and continued our climb, conducting mild maneuvers to check

Boeing President Bill Allen (bow tie) congratulates first 727 crew (in flight suits). On Allen's right is George Shairer, Vice President of Research and Development. Shairer was responsible for bringing Jack Steiner (facing Allen) to Boeing in the 1940s.

lateral control. After a few minutes we raised the landing gear. Then we continued handling maneuvers, getting the feel of the aircraft. Next, we began flap retraction, evaluating handling at each setting. We were unable to get the leading edge slats up because the actuators were too small for the loads — the reason the first flight photos show them extended.

"During the flight we flew the ship with hydraulics turned off then checked the other systems. We also did approaches to stalls and verified buffet speeds. As a result, we elected to use a normal reference approach speed rather than adding ten knots as had been suggested in the preflight briefing.

"After flying formation with the Constellation photo plane for PR pictures, we landed at Paine Field to end the first hop. We used Runway 34 with flaps extended to 40°, touching down right on reference speed. After landing, the spoilers were extended, brakes and reverse applied. The ground roll was amazingly short! I taxied to the ramp and parked near an extremely jubilant crowd including Boeing's president, Bill Allen, and the 727's standard-bearer, Jack Steiner. By this time I knew we had a winner and confidently told everyone so."

Loesch recalls, "I am a great believer in our American competitive system; it produces the best products. However, in some head-to-head aircraft competitions, there is so much at stake that corporate commitments on cost, weight and so on sometimes inhibit optimum engineering and construction. The 727 did not have a head-on competitive rival but it was born in the middle of the intense 707 vs. DC-8 battle. It demanded the very best of everyone, especially in view of its uniqueness and the controversies surrounding it. It was not hamstrung by commitments which required penalizing compromises. The timing was such that the airlines could and did make significant design suggestions, a vital factor for a healthy program. I believe all this led to the success of the 727.

"Although we had worked with the designers for long months prior to the first flight, the unique aerodynamic and propulsion features left unanswered questions, and led to some skepticism. Few of us realized what a fine airplane we had.

After a day of flight tests, the first 727 is inspected by ground-men on the wet Seattle ramp. Following the first ten hours of flight, conducted over open areas by federal requirement, the prototype was ferried to Boeing Field for further testing. The delighted first passenger on this hop — Jack Steiner.

The 707 prototype, seen here with the first two 727s completed, served to flight test the 727's flap system and rear engine configuration. It first flew on June 15, 1954, and completed two decades of test work before being donated to the National Air and Space Museum. It is currently stored in Arizona. The prototype 727 (N7001U) still flys in the colors of United Air Lines while N72700 remains a Boeing test vehicle.

"The weather at Renton was perfect for the first flight. We planned to land at Paine Field north of Seattle, where 747s are now built. The only real problem encountered was surging of the center engine. It was immediately obvious that the airplane had superior handling qualities.

"My wife and two small sons rode with a nervous vice president from Renton to Paine and from her description of the wild trip, I am sure I was much safer on the 727!

"The center engine problem stemmed from a faulty surge bleed valve and was corrected before the second flight. The loud report heard right after takeoff worried Jack Steiner, Joe Sutter and Ray Utterstrom, Sutter and Utterstrom being technical design engineers on Steiner's team. The three jumped into a small aircraft to follow us. They breathed a sigh of relief when the problem was discovered to be minor."

Two hours and one minute after takeoff, the first 727 flight ended and there was much celebration. The Seattle *Post Intelligencer* pictured Boeing's new baby on page one with the banner headline, "SHE'S OFF — OUR NEW BOEING!" The Seattle *Times* reported, ". . . like a caged bird reveling in the new-found freedom of the skies, the fledgling Boeing 727 soared over Puget Sound on its maiden flight yesterday to herald a new phase in air travel."

Every year on February 9, Wallick, Loesch and Shulenberger get together for lunch — and to talk about that memorable day in 1963.

Jane's Introduction

JANE'S ALL THE WORLD'S AIRCRAFT, long recognized as *the* authority on machines that take wing, succinctly announced the Boeing 727 in its 1962-63 edition as follows:

THE BOEING MODEL 727

"In early December, 1960, Boeing announced its intention to produce a new short/medium-range jet transport designated Boeing 727. A major innovation, compared with this company's earlier designs, is the choice of a rear-engined layout, with two Pratt & Whitney JT8D-1 turbofan engines mounted on the sides of the rear fuselage and a third at the base of the T-tail assembly.

In other respects the 727 will bear a close resemblance to the 707 and 720 series. It will have an identical upper fuselage section and many parts and systems will be interchangeable between the three types.

Simultaneously with the Boeing announcement, Eastern and United Air Lines each signed agreements to purchase 40 Model 727's. In February, 1961, Lufthansa ordered 12, and on August 10 American Airlines signed a contract for the purchase of 25. T.W.A. ordered 10 in March, 1962. The prototype is expected to fly in January, 1963. Deliveries are scheduled to begin late in 1963."

TYPE. — Three-engined jet airliner.

WINGS. — Cantilever low-wing monoplane. Aspect ratio 7.67. Chord 20 ft. 6 in. (6.25 m.) at root, 7 ft. 7.6 in. (2.32 m.) at tip. Dihedral 3°. Incidence 2°. Sweepback at 25% chord 32°. All-metal two-spar structure, passing through fuselage. Aluminium-alloy skin stiffened by aluminium stringers supports most of the bending loads. Removable wing-tips. Hydraulically-powered ailerons, in inboard (high-speed) and outboard (low-speed) units, operate in conjunction with spoilers. Outboard spoilers also function as air-brakes. Triple-slotted trailing-edge flaps. Full-span leading-edge retractable slats (outboard) and Krueger flaps (inboard). Thermal anti-icing of leading-edges. Total area of ailerons 75 sq. ft. (6.97m.²). Total area of flaps 281 sq. ft. (26.1 m.²). Gross wing area 1,650 sq. ft. (153.3 m²).

FUSELAGE. — Semi-monocoque structure, with aluminium-alloy skin and stringers over Z-type frames. Width 12 ft. 4 in. (3.76 m.). Depth (forward) 13 ft. 2 in. (4.0 m.). Depth (aft) 14 ft. (4.27 m.).

TAIL UNIT. — Cantilever monoplane type, with tailplane near tip of fin. Tailplane is of variable-incidence type. Dual rud-

ders with trim tabs. Hydraulically-powered control surfaces. Thermal anti-icing of leading-edges. Areas: vertical surfaces 290 sq. ft. (26.94 m.²), horizontal surfaces 376 sq. ft. (34.93 m.²). Tailplane span 35 ft. 5 in. (10.80 m).

LANDING GEAR. — Retractable tricycle type. Hydraulic retraction. Main units retract inboard into fuselage. Oleo-pneumatic shock-absorbers. Twin wheels on all units. Steerable nose-wheel. Main wheel tyres size 49 X 17. Nose-wheel tyres size 32 X 11.5. Brakes on all wheels, with anti-skid devices. Wheel track 18 ft. 9 in. (5.72 m.). Wheelbase 53 ft. 3 in. (16.23 m.).

POWER PLANT. — Three 14,000 lb. (6.350 kg.) s.t. Pratt & Whitney JT8D-1 turbofan engines, with thrust reversers. Each has individual fuel system fed from integral tank in wings, but all three tanks are interconnected. Basic total fuel capacity 7,000 U.S. gallons (26,500 litres).

ACCOMMODATION. — Crew of three on flight deck. Normal accommodation for 70 first-class passengers in four-abreast seats with centre aisle. 114 tourist-class in six-abreast seats, or a mixed-class version with 28 first-class and 66 tourist. Two central galleys and wardrobes. Toilets at front (1) and rear (2). Entry via hydraulically-actuated integral aft stairway and optional Weber Aircraft electrically-operated airstairs at front of cabin on port side. Length of cabin 72 ft. 8 in. (22.15 m.). Pressure differential of 8.6 lb./sq. in. (0.60 kg/cm.²) makes possible sea level cabin pressure up to 22,500 ft. (6,850 m). Full air-conditioning system. Two heated and pressurised baggage and freight compartments under floor, each with a 2 ft. 11. in. X 4 ft. (0.89 X 1.22 m.) door. Capacities: front 340 cub. ft. (9.63 m³), rear 510 cub. ft. (14.44 m³). Comprehensive equipment includes provision for Doppler and Sperry Phoenix SP-50 automatic flight control system.

One of many seating arrangements for the 727-100 is this 114-passenger, all-coach version.

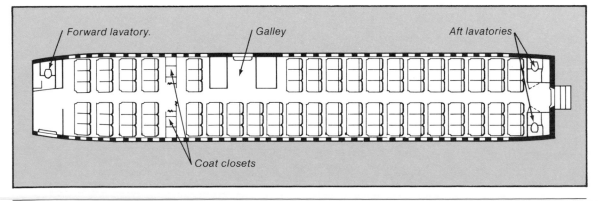

Forward lavatory.   Galley   Aft lavatories

Coat closets

DIMENSIONS.—

Span	108 ft. 7 in. (33·10 m)
Overall length	132 ft. 5 in. (40·35 m)
Length of fuselage	114 ft. 10 in. (35·0 m)
Height	34 ft. (10·36 m)

WEIGHTS AND LOADINGS. —

Operating weight empty	81,000 lb (36,740 kg)
Max. payload	24,000 lb (10,886 kg)
Max T.O. weight	142,000 lb (64,410 kg)
Max. ramp weight	143,000 lb (64,860 kg)
Max. zero-fuel weight	109,000 lb (49,440 kg)
Max. landing weight	131,000 lb (59,420 kg)
Max. wing loading	86 lb/sq ft (420 kg/m^2)
Max. power loading	3·3 lb/lb st (3·3 kg/kg st)

PERFORMANCE (estimated). —

Max. cruising speed	Mach 0·88 or 580 mph (933 kmh)
Time to 25,000 ft (7,620 m)	10 min.
CAR T.O. runway length	5,000 ft (1,525 m)
CAR landing runway length	5,000 ft (1,525 m)
Range with max. fuel, SR-427A reserves	1,700 miles (2,735 km)

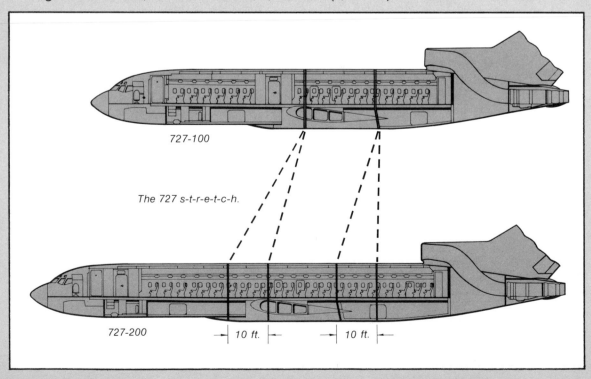

727-100

The 727 s-t-r-e-t-c-h.

727-200 |← 10 ft. |← |← 10 ft. |←

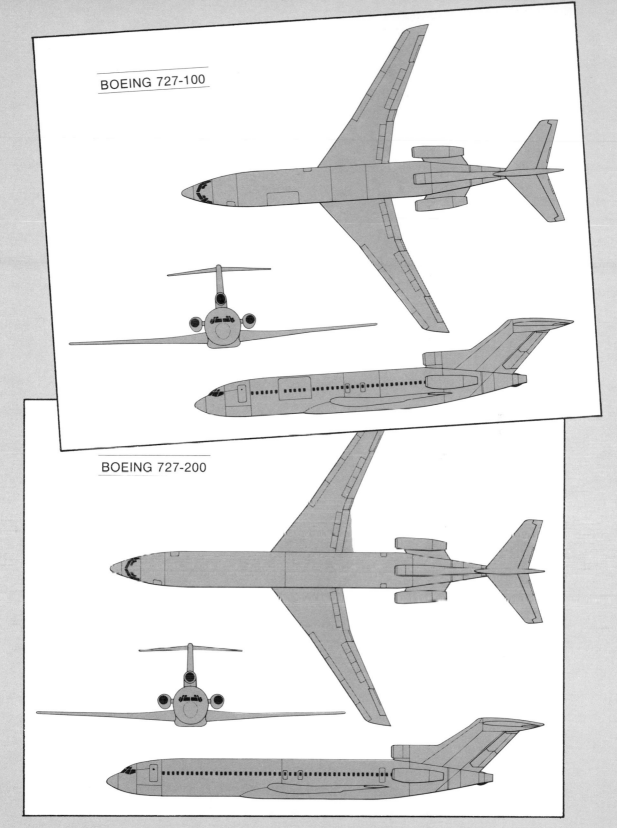

BOEING 727-100

BOEING 727-200

A comparison in sizes. The 727-100 first flew on February 9, 1963, the -200 on July 27, 1967. Only the -100 has been built with optional large cargo door. Except for the obvious difference in fuselage length, the two models seem identical to the casual observer. Yet, note the cabin doors installed just ahead of Engines 1 and 3 on the stretched version. And note in the head-on views the center engine scoops; the -100 scoop is oval while the -200's is round. The 727-200 is three inches longer than the largest 707 built.

The 727?

It could as easily have been the 726 or 728. *Seven-Twenty-Seven* it became by chance. The background is interesting.

On July 27, 1949, an unusual aircraft rose from Hatfield Aerodrome on the outskirts of London and climbed rapidly into the warm air, trailing smoke. It was deHavilland Model 106, the *Comet,* making its maiden flight. This milestone left handwriting on the wall though not all airliner builders paused to read the words. The implications were not lost on Boeing's engineers who already knew a thing or two about large jets, having launched their own twice-as-big B-47 bomber a year and a half earlier. Even to the layman it is obvious that a big plane is a big plane whether it hauls bombs or people. Rework

The graceful Comet, first of all jet airliners.

the fuselage and bomber becomes airliner, or vice versa; it's been done many times. Quite naturally, the Seattle designers watched the deHavilland with keen interest and thought their own thoughts.

Realizing that the piston-powered transport had reached its zenith, they earlier had begun studies to improve Model 367, military version of Model 377, the double-decked *Stratocruiser.* Eventually, the eightieth configuration of Model 367 was approved for construction. It was a large four-jet, swept-wing transport looking nothing at all like the ship on which the studies had begun. The new product was rolled out and flown as Model 367-80, however, and kept the designation throughout its eventful life as a test vehicle.

The brand new airplane deserved a brand new identity so the 700 series of model numbers was selected for a new line of commercial products. Thus, the first production copy of 367-80 was stamped "707." Old "Dash Eighty" has been re-

The Boeing 377, best remembered
as the Stratocruiser.

tired and given to the National Air and Space Museum, by the
way. The later 720, though similar in appearance to the 707, is
in fact much lighter, tailored for work on medium-distance
routes and individual enough to rate its own label. The three-
engine 727 and twin-engine 737 are still later original designs
bearing but a family resemblance to their larger sisters and the
747, needless to note, occupies a stage unshared with kin or
competitors.

In an attempt to name its first jet airliner, Boeing introduced
the 707 as the *Jet Stratoliner,* but it never caught on with the
press or public. The 720, 727, 747 and 737 came out by the
numbers. Americans name their cars and number their planes

"Jet Clipper David Crockett," a
727-100 poses with big brother,
"Clipper Westwind," a 747-121.

The Boeing 737, dubbed "Fluf" by airline pilots. Why? Ask an airline pilot.

for reasons unexplained. Surprisingly, the British, who throughout World War II and for years after gave names to the U. S. types they flew, have not popularized any of the Boeing jet airliners.

Among airline crews, on this side at least, the 707 and 727 are often referred to as the "Four Holer" and "Three Holer", though whether this stems from the respective numbers of tailpipes is uncertain. The 707 has four toilets, the 727 three, and many of the first pilots to fly them grew up on the farm. The 737 has more than once been called "Fluf" for whatever reason and the monstrous 747 is to many of its admiring crewmen, "Fat Al."

Production

Sub-contracted parts for the 727 are fabricated and forwarded to Seattle for assembly. Almost every state is represented plus several foreign countries. California tops the list of states supplying components, from the on-board auxiliary power unit to tiny sensors monitoring temperatures and pressures. The fuel tanks come from Vermont, the engines are built in Connecticut and the escape slides are test-inflated in New Jersey. The cabin windows are made in Australia while some radio equipment is Italian. The auto-pilot and radar are from deep in the heart of Texas.

...in any colors!

Braniff gets you there
with Flying Colors . . .

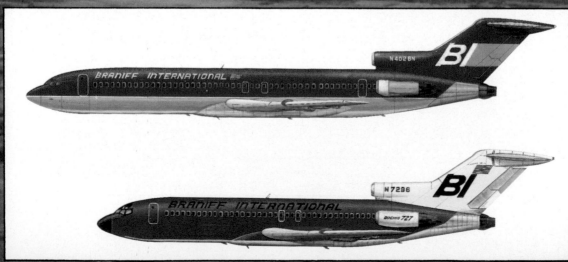

Reminiscent of the interior of a railroad president's private car, this plushed-out 727 is one of several conversions serving as capitalist tools for major corporations and influential individuals alike. Conference rooms, staterooms with shower stalls and a galley that would be the envy of even the most discerning chef are all standard equipment if this modification is selected.

Flying the Three-Holer

An old saw is that an airplane may disappoint a good pilot but it will never surprise him. It's good to think on that when you sit down to work in a 727 for the ship is so superbly engineered and well built that its very reliability can pose a problem. How easy it is to slip from the knowledge that it probably *won't* play nasty tricks to the cheerful notion that it *can't.*

The next thing is to get comfortable. Each seat adjusts more ways than a barber's chair for it is important to see what's going on inside and out without moving more than the head. The arrangement is customary with pilot on the left, copilot on the right and flight engineer behind. Call them captain, first officer and second officer and don't always expect to see *males* at their posts.

On the ground the 727 is a rather clumsy vehicle, driven like a truck — a truck 153 feet long and 108 feet wide, that is. Rolling straight ahead is easy but tight turns require extreme caution as the main wheels are way back there cutting across the circle. Since the 727 puts more weight on its mains per/ square inch of tire than even the giant 747, you will go in to the hubcaps if you get them in the grass. Nothing to do then but shut down, call for buses to collect the passengers and wonder how the interview with the chief pilot will go. Such nightmarish possibilities make pilots knock on wood — and taxi carefully.

Getting away from the gate at some stations offers equal risk of embarrassment because jet blast is high enough to damage passenger loaders and terminal plate glass. Compared to navigating the labyrinth of taxiways at Kennedy on a rainy night, the subsequent hop to Atlanta is a piece of cake.

Since jet engines are ready to work the minute they are lit, you can launch upon reaching the runway, traffic permitting.

Checklists are read on the way out and the engineer goes to his books with the final weights of passengers, freight and fuel to find the "numbers" — wing flap and trim settings, speeds for takeoff and climb. Lined up on the runway, you advance the three thrust levers an inch, wait for all engines to spin up, then work them forward until takeoff power registers on the gauges. The copilot attends to their fine tuning and the engineer keeps an eye on the twenty-five or so readings that report engine health. Acceleration is good, all things considered, and soon you're pounding along the rough concrete at race car speed, observing with interest the approaching end of the concrete.

"Rotate," calls out the copilot, meaning you're fast enough to fly and you ease back on the wheel to pull the nose up eight degrees — no more, or the tail skid may drag. The ship hangs right there for a moment, half truck, half plane, then the mains break free with the slight thump of extending struts and you're flying. Seconds later he calls, "Positive rate of climb," and you call for gear up. The doors open, the wheels come up, the doors close and little lights on the panel flick on and off to confirm these operations. The controls become firmer with increasing speed and now there is some wind noise about the cockpit. At a thousand feet, you call for climb power and flaps up on schedule, nailing speed on 250 knots, the limit below 10,000 feet, doing these and a dozen other routine chores subconsciously, your concentration being upon the broad

Left: A line of thundershowers ahead are painting well on this tri-motor's radar and dictate a slight turn to the left to avoid raising white-caps on the customers' pre-dinner cocktails.

complex traffic picture of which your trip is but a minor part.

Forty-five minutes after push back, you are seven miles above sea level, doing 80% of the speed of sound and surrounded by scores of instruments which tell you all the right stories. The autopilot performs faultlessly; the ride is so smooth your seat seems set in concrete and the illusion is that the plane is motionless while the gray remote landscape below inches slowly past. Until descent begins two hours from now, you three are monitors rather than pilots and engineer, watching splendid machinery do its own thing in its own way with but occasional prompting by human hands. During such tranquil periods, with fresh coffee in hand, you find yourself once again admiring this sterling craft known as the 727.

It is easy to learn and a delight to handle. It is sensible, predictable, trustworthy, reliable and as stout-hearted as an oak clipper. History seems likely to accord it the same distinction among jet airliners as the redoubtable DC-3 earned in the piston age.

Time to start down. When the proper milage shows in the DME window, you retard thrust levers to idle and gently nose over to keep speed at Mach .80 to milk the last pound of thrust from the last pound of fuel. Speed is reduced to 250 before reaching 10,000 and to 200 as you are vectored onto final approach. Four miles from the runway you call for flaps two and await the green light that says they are down. Then it's flaps five and wait again. Green light — now you know all

leading edge slats and flaps are extended and that further extension of the trailing edge flaps may be made as speed diminishes. Flaps fifteen and speed back to 150, then call for gear down. Doors open, wheels fold out, doors close and three greens say you've got all three legs extended and locked in place. Flaps twenty-five, flaps thirty and speed at ten knots above the "reference speed" for your weight.

All that remains is the landing. Few aviation terms have more meanings than "landing." The idea is to convert graceful flyer into awkward truck as smoothly as possible, to roll it on, to get a greaser, a paint job with ground contact as subtle as the wet slap of brush against board fence. It is not a difficult exercise but it requires concentration, attention to detail, favorable conditions and a little bit of luck. For all this, a firm arrival is sometimes the reward. The 727 does not embarrass a pilot as often as the Electra or flatter him as often as the 707. With the mains rolling, raise the spoilers, lower the nose and pull in reverse thrust. At 80 knots, ease out of reverse and use brakes sparingly. Taxi to the terminal, ease into the gate, shut down engines and secure the cockpit.

Pilot admiration does not stem from easy going in ideal conditions but from the way the ship handles and performs when the work gets hard. The 727 is a good instrument airplane, meaning it is stable in rough air and responsive during approach when flight is conducted in cloud. It is manageable in gusty crosswinds and can be brought to a stop on short run-

ways. It is designed to tolerate mechanical breakdown with minimum effect on safety. It can fly indefinitely on two engines and, in fact, is routinely ferried to maintenance facilities on two, though no passengers are carried. It can remain aloft on one engine long enough to reach a suitable airport. Its engines are so reliable that many a pilot has never experienced a failure in scheduled operations.

Four pumps supply hydraulic pressure to operate landing gear, flaps, brakes and other devices and any one can do all the work. If all failed, the gear will free fall, flaps can be extended electrically and air used for braking. A landing with flaps retracted and no brakes is safe enough if you pick the right runway. There are three generators, any one of which can power essential flight instruments and radio gear.

That the 727 is popular with its crews is of more than passing interest. Pilots and engineers who are comfortable in an airplane and confident in their abilities to fly it on all-weather schedules are sure to do the safest job.

And that's what it's all about.

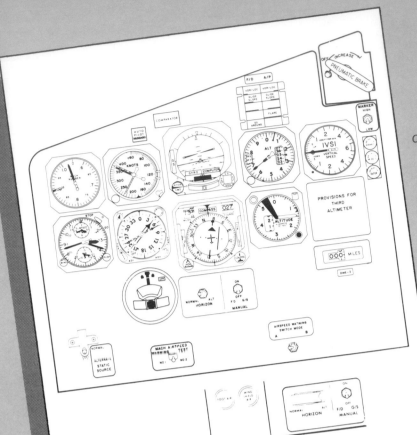

Captain's flight instruments.

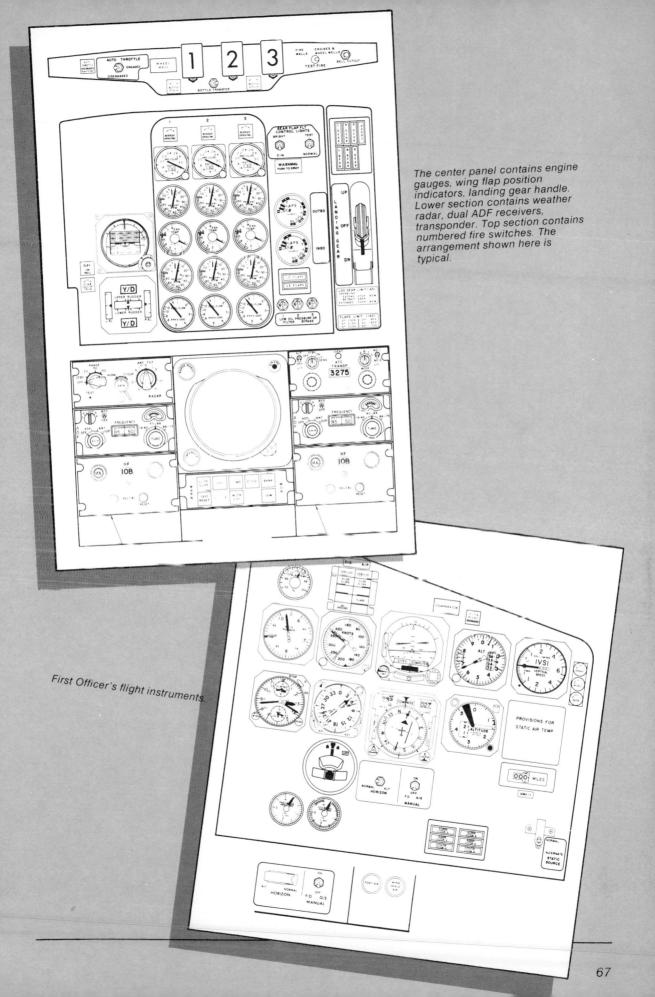

The center panel contains engine gauges, wing flap position indicators, landing gear handle. Lower section contains weather radar, dual ADF receivers, transponder. Top section contains numbered fire switches. The arrangement shown here is typical.

First Officer's flight instruments.

The Systems

Crewmen qualifying to fly an airliner must gain a thorough knowledge of its several systems. Intensive ground schooling is followed by simulator and flight training. Normal, abnormal and emergency procedures are explored in detail, the program culminating in written and oral exams then practical demonstrations observed by company and federal inspectors. Among the topics covered in 727 school are:

Powerplants — three P&W turbofans supply thrust. Each has two rotors in series labeled N_1 and N_2 which, at maximum output, spin at 8,600 and 12,250 rpms respectively. The engines are referred to as Numbers 1, 2 and 3, left to right facing forward. Numbers 1 and 2 turn hydraulic pumps; all three turn generators. The engines also supply heat for wing and cowl anti-icing, pressure air for air conditioning and pressurization.

Fuel — three main tanks in wings and center section contain (in a typical 727-200) 54,511 pounds of fuel, or 8,106 gallons, jet fuel weighing about 6.7 pounds per gallon at 60°F. Takeoff is made "tank-to-engine," each engine drawing fuel from its own tank; in flight any combination of engines can draw from any combination of tanks. Fuel can be dumped at the rate of 2,350 pounds per minute down to 2,500 pounds per tank should it become necessary to land before normal burnoff reduces gross weight to the legal landing maximum.

Hydraulics — two engine-driven and two electric pumps supply pressure for operation of landing gear, flaps, spoilers, flight controls and other purposes. A fifth standby pump is available to power one rudder and extend leading edge flaps should main system pressure fail. Trailing edge flaps are electrically extended if hydraulics become inoperative.

Electrical — each AC generator powers its own bus. Normally the generators are operated in parallel, their buses coupled. Each has a constant speed drive to keep output steady regardless of engine speed. Any CSD can be disconnected in flight, the remaining two generators picking up its load through the bus tie circuit. Electrical power in employed in hundreds of ways, from heating coffee to wiping windshields.

Flight controls — the 727 has two rudders, four ailerons, fourteen spoiler sections and twenty-six flap panels, all hydraulically boosted. Tabs are provided for roll and directional trim, the electrically-powered stabilizer working in the vertical axis through thumb switches on the control wheels.

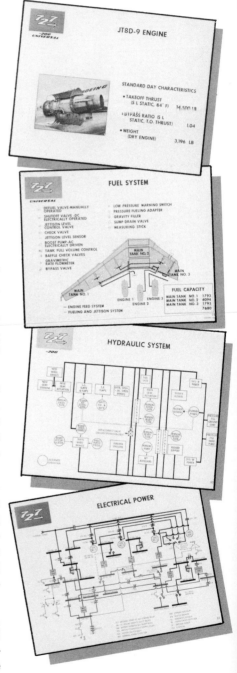

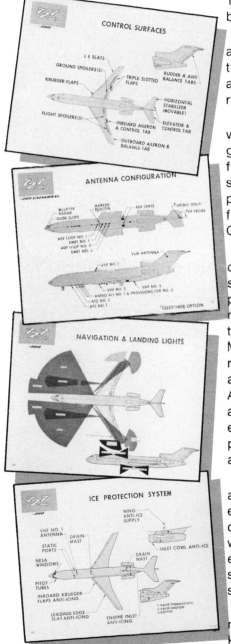

The aircraft is flyable with all "power steering" out and stabilizer jammed.

Communications — three VHF transceivers are standard aboard domestic 727s to provide contact with radar controllers and company stations. Dual VOR/ILS/DME/ADF apparatus is installed for navigation and a 300-mile weather radar set is standard equipment.

Air conditioning and pressurization — two "packs" in the wing roots mix ram air with compressor output bled from engines to keep cabin atmosphere safe and comfortable at all flight levels. Maximum cabin pressure is 8.6 pounds per square inch, allowing cabin altitude to remain at sea level pressure when the aircraft is flying at 24,000 feet; at 39,000 feet, cabin altitude is 7,000 feet, about the altitude of Mexico City.

Instrumentation — each pilot faces an identical but independently-fed set of flight instruments showing altitude, attitude, speed, rate of climb and so on. Other gauges on the forward panel and engineer's large display record engine readings, monitor all systems and provide such useful data as temperatures inside and out, flap position, cabin altitude and pressure. Much information is provided by lights of several colors which report rising temperatures or falling pressures or quantities and others which verify that valves are opening or closing. And there are bells, horns, rattles, buzzers and chimes to alert, remind, confirm, prompt or sound a warning. There's even a taped voice which says, "Glide slope," if landing approach is too low or "Pull up! pull up!" if descent is too rapid at low level.

Other systems — the automatic flight system enables the autopilot to follow airway signals to a destination, then execute an approach to 100 feet; fire protection for engines and cabin fires; ice and rain protection (windshields, pitot masts, wings, engine inlets, etc.); oxygen for crew and passengers; emergency gear including a fire axe, crank for manual extension of the wheels, first aid kits, escape windows, ropes and slides, megaphones, rafts and life vests.

Once these subjects are mastered, candidates learn how to manage the complex machinery in day-to-day flying in all kinds of weather.

Simulator technicians examine minature airport "seen" by TV camera rolling on rails to left.

Back to School

Twice a year a 727 captain straps himself into the left seat knowing that just about everything that can go wrong with his airplane *will* go wrong before the day is over. A score of serious problems — from loss of an engine's power at the critical moment of lift off to wing flaps that refuse to extend — are certain to confront him during the schedule about to begin. He can only guess, however, at the order in which the nightmarish situations will occur. He is about to get a proficiency check and will not actually fly in the process, the entire exercise taking place indoors in a clever device called a flight simulator.

One of the things that sets an airline pilot apart from his non-flying friends is the requirement that he periodically prove that he remains as good at his work as the day he got the job. Copilots and engineers are called in once a year, captains semiannually. It all begins when a 60-question exam appears in a crewman's mailbox along with a schedule for groundschool and simulator period. The completed questionnaire (00 is passing) must be turned in when reporting for the day of classroom study. The simulator ride comes a week or so later and is best preceded by a thorough review of aircraft manuals.

This phase of recurrent training is conducted by a check airman, a company pilot called in from the line to give flight instruction and proficiency checks, this status itself requiring federal approval. Do not imagine for an instant that the fact your simulator instructor is an acquaintance of long standing, perhaps even a man with whom you once flew for months as captain or copilot, will have the slightest influence on the outcome. The atmosphere in airline training and checking is friendly but strictly business. Check airmen are generally more difficult to please than FAA inspectors who, incidentally, often sit in on simulator rides. You have got to get it done right, no matter who is back there observing.

The session gets under way in a classroom where the instructor reviews the normal, abnormal and emergency procedures required in the check, asking enough questions to determine if his two students are prepared. Then to the simulator, a large cylindrical affair which from outside roughly resembles the nose section of a 727. Inside it is identical, from seat belts to ash trays. It sits on struts which provide enough motion to enhance the illusion of flight. The pilots take their places with the instructor on the jump seat behind. At the

engineer's panel sits a student ready to wrestle with malfunctions presented by his own instructor.

You learn to to do this . . .

The checklists are read and engines started, the exhaust gas temperature of one probably soaring toward the danger point, requiring immediate shut down. Few pilots have seen an actual "over-temp," but it can happen and it is worthwhile to review the immediate action necessary to prevent serious damage. The second start is normal. Then the instructor issues a typical departure clearance, for example, "After take-off, climb to 4,000 feet on runway heading, then turn left and proceed direct to such-and-such a VOR station, to hold east; maintain 7,000 feet." Beyond the windshields stretches what appears to be a long runway. Actually, it is a screen displaying the image seen by a TV camera poised at the end of a toy runway on a huge model airport in another room of the training building. It is synchronized with the simulator's flight controls and follows exactly the student's race down the strip — or ignominious swerve off into the grass if he loses control, but no harm is done by such a blunder. The instructor can freeze all action with the flip of a switch and return the embarrassed student to the end of the runway for another try.

Brakes are released, power advanced and the takeoff begins again. The airspeed needles climb to 60, to 80, to 100, runway lights flash past on either side and the simulator rumbles as though real tires are rapidly rolling across real concrete. Just prior to rotation speed, the engineer calls out, "Power loss on Number Two!" The captain slams the thrust

. . . in one of these.

levers closed, grabs the speed brake handle, pulls Engines One and Three into maximum reverse and brakes hard. The end of the runway is just beyond the nose when all motion stops. "Very nice," says the instructor. An engine failure during takeoff, like a hot start, is an extremely remote possibility, something a pilot may never see in routine flying, but it remains a possibility and one which demands immediate instinctive response for successful solution. And, like most unusual situations, it is not something you can practice with a load of passengers. All the more reason for periodic review.

During his hour and a half at the controls, a captain will experience a wide range of nasty problems — a wheel well fire caused by overheated brakes, an engine failure, a short circuit which fills the cockpit with smoke (imaginary, not real; simulation doesn't go that far!), dutch rolling caused by loss of yaw dampers, loss of pressurization requiring an emergency descent, loss of all hydraulic fluid which calls for cranking the wheels down and electric flap extension, loss of all generator power, a jammed stabilizer and so on.

It is not a case of sitting there in straight and level flight, wondering what dirty trick will be pulled out of the bag next. A proficiency check includes a number of instrument approaches to an airport reporting minimum weather conditions and the problems arise during these maneuvers in whatever order the instructor desires. For instance, the student may be nearing the airport and setting up for an ILS approach when an engine fails. He must continue the approach while supervising the

This is the "airport" . . .

engine shut down procedure, and he may descend to 100 feet, the legal minimum altitude, only to find that conditions have deteriorated to the point that the runway cannot be seen. With nothing ahead but the clammy whiteness of fog (the simulator does this extremely well), there is no alternative but to pour on the coal, retract flaps and gear and climb back to a safe level — on two engines. Circling for another try, a second engine fails, calling for an entirely different approach technique. This time the ceiling lifts a bit and a normal landing is made. Then it is back to the end of the runway for another departure and approach with assorted headaches along the way. It is a long-ish afternoon.

A copilot must perform the same maneuvers and cope with the same problems during his own test, though he flies from the right seat. When a pilot fails to complete an exercise to the required standards, he repeats it until he gets it right. Only two grades are given in simulator work: "S" — satisfactory, and "U". The pilot who fumbles too many of the balls is scheduled for another check or for whatever training is needed to restore his proficiency. The average airline type works at his job in day to day flying and maintains the high degree of skill expected by his management and the government. While he hardly rel-ishes the thought of the next check, he tackles it with confi-dence.

A successful ride does not quite wrap it up for the next six months. Within the month he will get a line check with a check pilot occupying the jump seat for two legs of a routine trip to insure that a pilot's practice is as good as his theory. An FAA air carrier inspector may appear at any time, unannounced, to sit in on the game and see that it is being played strictly by the

. . . on which these simulator students are about to "land."

rules. This program of intensive training, periodic checking and continuous monitoring (everything said in an airliner cockpit and all radio contacts with ground stations are taped) is part of the life. Pilots sometimes suggest that the same philosophy, if followed in other professions, might produce similarly good results.

Until introduction of the flight simulator, flight training and check rides were accomplished in aircraft, often after midnight when a ship could be spared from schedules. It was an expensive business for the airlines and a hairy one for pilots. There were more accidents than the industry cares to remember. Riding in back, waiting your turn at 3:00 a.m., while a 707 struggled through a circling approach with two engines shut down on the same side made you fervently hope the check pilot up front was completely on top of the situation.

The savings in fuel alone is worth noting. One major line has watched the per gallon cost rise from 19¢ to 43¢ in four years, bringing the operating cost of a 727 to more than $800 an hour.

An airline large enough to justify the expense of buying and maintaining flight simulators keeps them in operation almost around the clock, training and checking its own crews by day and those of smaller lines by night. Indeed, this phase of airline work can generate a sizeable profit on its own.

Safety is the name of the game. Would you as a passenger have it any other way? For what it's worth, an airline pilot worries more when his wife drives to town than when she flies home with the kids to see Grandma.

He knows the score.

By the Numbers

You fly the 727 by the numbers. Its weight and balance, take-off performance, cruise power settings, flight plan data, descent schedule and landing speeds are computed and numerically displayed in the cockpit.

The tabulations begin before the engines are started. Armed with the final passenger, baggage and cargo count, the Flight Engineer totals these weights to arrive at the figure needed to calculate take-off speeds. He jots the numbers down on the "take-off data card" and passes it forward for the pilots to set with their airspeed bugs. Also noted is a contingent take-off safety speed necessary in the event of an engine failure. Engine power settings are given plus a reduced "standard power" selection that prolongs engine life and may be used under certain conditions.

The card is flipped over, and on the reverse side appears the landing data. The reference speed that considers the aircraft's landing weight is here plus local weather, airport con-

TYPICAL 727 LOADING: DFW–LGA

	WEIGHT	% OF TOTAL WEIGHT
*Basic Aircraft (727-200)	100,840 #	60%
Dispatch Fuel	36,000 #	22%
**Passenger Load	21,760 #	13%
***Passenger Baggage . .	3,136 #	2%
Cargo	5,560 #	3%
****Take-Off Weight	167,296 #	100%
Enroute Burn-Off	−23,100 #	−14%
*****Landing Weight	144,196 #	86%

*Includes crew with their baggage, engine oil, hydraulic fluid, meals for each seat, all galley equipment, all lavatory items but not any payload or fuel.

**128 x 170# / each (summer weights are five pounds lighter due to the absence of overcoats).

***128 x 24.5# (Standard, and this doesn't miss it far).

****The Flight Engineer figures the take-off speeds on this number.

*****In cruise at 37,000 feet, the 727 is burning fuel at the rate of 7,800# / hour and thus getting lighter by 130# per minute!

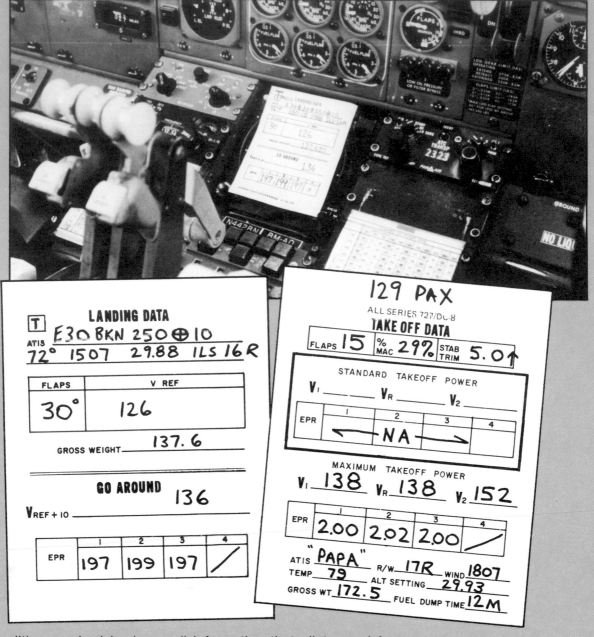

LANDING DATA

T

ATIS E30 BKN 250 ⊕ 10

72° 1507 29.88 ILS 16R

FLAPS	V REF
30°	126

GROSS WEIGHT _____ 137.6 _____

GO AROUND 136

V_{REF} + 10 _____

	1	2	3	4
EPR	197	199	197	/

129 PAX

ALL SERIES 727/DC-8

TAKE OFF DATA

FLAPS 15 %MAC 29% STAB TRIM 5.0↑

STANDARD TAKEOFF POWER

V_1 ____ V_R ____ V_2 ____

EPR	1	2	3	4
	← — NA — →			

MAXIMUM TAKEOFF POWER

V_1 138 V_R 138 V_2 152

EPR	1	2	3	4
	2.00	2.02	2.00	/

ATIS "PAPA" R/W 17R WIND 1807

TEMP 79 ALT SETTING 29.93

GROSS WT 172.5 FUEL DUMP TIME 12M

ditions and advisories — all information that pilots need for landing.

And in cruise it's no different. Pilots refer to what appears to be a maze of confusing numbers on a digital flight plan that deals in ''real time'' data. That is, the latest winds and weather along the route are fed into the computer along with actual passenger and cargo loads. Pilots have current information pertaining to *their* flight to help in the selection of the best altitude and route for the smoothest ride for their passengers and the most fuel efficient trip for their company.

With fuel prices soaring, the computer considers many factors before advising the pilot how to stretch the most miles out of each pound of fuel. And pilots lean heavily on profile descents that allow them to remain at economical altitudes until the last possible moment before starting down for landing. All by the numbers.

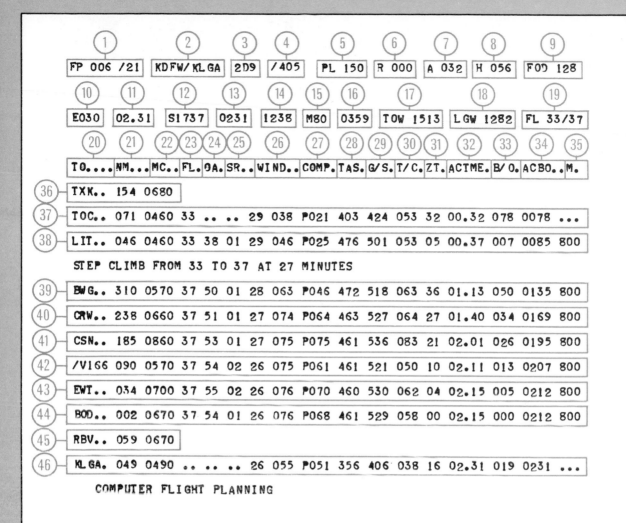

COMPUTER FLIGHT PLAN LEGEND

1. Flight number / date
2. Point of departure / destination (Dallas–Ft. Worth to New York's La Guardia)
3. Aircraft type and engine installed (727-200 with JT8D-9 engines)
4. Aircraft number
5. Payload (passengers + baggage + cargo)
6. Fuel reserves planned
7. Fuel to alternate planned
8. Fuel to hold, if necessary
9. Fuel over destination (Take off fuel less enroute burn-off)
10. Computer code
11. Time enroute (Take-off to touchdown)
12. Cost of trip
13. Fuel burn for trip
14. Nautical mileage
15. Designated Mach number to be flown
16. Take-off fuel
17. Take-off gross weight
18. Gross weight on landing
19. Cruising altitudes (Flight level 330 then step climb to flight level 370)
20. First checkpoint of trip (TO is the take-off)
21. Nautical mileage between checkpoints
22. Magnetic course between checkpoints
23. Flight level
24. Outside air temperature at altitude
25. Shear factor (Predictable turbulence; 1 is light to none while 5 is heavy)
26. Wind direction at cruising altitude
27. Velocity of wind
28. Expected true airspeed if temperature is as forecast
29. Expected ground speed in knots
30. True course
31. Zone time (time between checkpoints)
32. Accumulated zone time
33. Fuel burn-off between checkpoints
34. Accumulated fuel burn-off
35. Cruise Mach number
36. Checkpoint — Texarkana, Texas
37. Checkpoint — top of climb
38. Checkpoint — Little Rock, Arkansas
39. Checkpoint — Bowling Green, Kentucky
40. Checkpoint — Charleston, West Virginia
41. Checkpoint — Casanova, Virginia
42. Checkpoint — intersection of another airway
43. Checkpoint — New Castle, Delaware
44. Checkpoint — beginning of descent
45. Checkpoint — Robbinsville, New Jersey
46. Destination — La Guardia Airport

Third Man Up Front

Soon after World War II, the CAA (now FAA) ruled that airliners larger than the DC-4 must carry a "flight engineer" during scheduled passenger operations. The new man was to concern himself with mechanical matters, freeing pilot and copilot to devote full attention to flying the increasingly congested airways.

Actually, there was nothing new about the idea. Mechanics were carried aboard airships and large bombers during World

Not all airline crewmembers are male. Meet Sandy Simmons, first of four young ladies to be hired by Braniff International to fill second officer positions. The mother of two daughters, Simmons recently upgraded to first officer.

War I, brave souls who walked along icy wings in midwinter to repair leaking fuel lines. Many big planes built between the wars carried engineers and the crews of most large bomber and transport types of World War II included an enlisted "crew chief" worth his weight in gold in emergency situations. The wings of some large piston aircraft — the B-36, for example — contained crawlways through which a crew chief could reach engines for minor adjustments.

Some of the first flight engineers hired by American carriers were licensed mechanics with no piloting experience. Today's second officer is a pilot who has earned an FAA Flight Engineer's Rating. He will upgrade to first officer and eventually captain as his seniority permits. In the meantime, while he sweats out the retirements and schedule expansions that lead to promotion, he is one busy fellow at his cockpit panel.

A 727 S/O's work day begins one hour before scheduled departure when he meets with his pilots to discuss the flight plan, determine fuel weight and proposed payload. Then he goes to the gate to meet the inbound trip and learn from its engineer what problems need immediate attention and which can be deferred. Next he makes a thorough walkaround inspection, checking the airframe for damage from bird strikes or ground equipment, alert for leaking plumbing in the wheel wells, telltale drips from fuel tanks or engines, loose inspection doors. The brakes are examined for wear, the tires for cuts or other damage. All navigation lights and rotating beacons are checked.

The cabin emergency gear is inspected — portable oxygen bottles and masks, first aid kits, fire extinguishers, megaphones, escape windows and, before overwater hops, rafts and life vests. In the cockpit he expects to find a fire axe, hand crank for manual extension of the landing gear, portable oxygen equipment, load manuals, log books and all the right pressures and quantities showing on a dozen gauges. He verifies that flight plan fuel is in fact in the tanks and properly distributed. He tests the engine fire warning system, his own quick-don mask and radios and obtains from the company station the correct time and altimeter setting.

He preflights his large panel of switches and instruments, verifying that fuel valves open and close, circuit breakers are in, air conditioning valves properly adjusted, pressurization controls set for the proposed cruising altitude. When the pilots come aboard he reads their checklists to them, doublechecking as they prepare their own equipment for flight.

During engine start he monitors engine indicators on his own panel and the pilots' instrument display, then he shuts down the auxiliary power unit. He radios the company operator to secure the final count of passengers and weights of

Right: The Second Officer's office. The fellow who brought this trip in was obviously unhappy with the reading of No. 1 oil quantity and maintenance is changing the gauge. But for the S/O, the two pilots would have to monitor and operate all of this gear with subsequent effect on their flying performance.

baggage, freight and mail. The load manual contains a separate page of calculations for each runway at every airfield served by the airline. From this chart the takeoff "numbers" arc determined — rotation and climb speeds, stabilizer and flap settings — due consideration being given to total weight, runway condition, wind, weather and other factors. These figures are jotted down on the takeoff data card and passed forward to the pilots. An experienced engineer can complete these computations and have all ship systems ready for launch by the time his trip reaches the end of the runway.

During takeoff he monitors engine performance, calling to the captain's attention any deviations from normal operation. In cruise he manages fuel burn, keeps an eye on engines and systems, completes log sheets for the entire crew, reports position to the company once an hour and placates the cabin attendants, half of whom say they are freezing while the rest want to know why he's keeping temperature so high. He's a jack of all trades and a master of all of them. "I've got the third best job in the world," he'll tell you.

Maximum takeoff weight no longer determines which airliners need engineers, each type now being judged on its own merits with cockpit workload the main consideration. There is much argument among manufacturers, airline officials and pilot groups as to the need for an engineer aboard this or that new type. The precarious economic picture in recent years has required much belt-tightening and made the two-man airliner all the more attractive to managements. Pilots maintain that there is a point beyond which the third cockpit crewmember is a necessity. But where to draw the line — total weight? Speed? Number of seats? Complexity of the routes to be flown? The concerned parties are far from agreement on the issue.

The vast majority of airline pilots opt for the three-man cockpit crew. They point to the 727's remarkable safety record as ample proof of the value of the young fellow who rides sideways behind the drivers, keeping a watchful eye on their plane — and them. As one put it, "He's cheap insurance."

"Before start checklist completed, Captain. All door lights out, pressure's up, beacon on, "A" System pumps off, ground interconnect closed, brakes off, standing by for engine start."

"Turn Number One — and tell the girls we're going to be about fifteenth in line for takeoff and see if you can promote a round of coffee, will you?"

Not in the Flight Plan

Airline crews are trained to handle a wide range of abnormal and emergency in-flight situations — engine failure, loss of pressurization, electrical or hydraulic problems, fire in the cabin or cargo bins, brake failure — the list of unpleasant possibilities is long and there is a procedure to follow in each case. Once in a long, long while something happens aboard an airliner which isn't in the books; there is no recommended procedure to follow because it never happened before. Here are three such incidents involving 727s:

On August 8, 1973, Braniff Flight 104, operating between Washington and New York with seventy-five passengers aboard, was just about to level off at its cruising altitude when it was violently rocked by an explosion. Captain Jack Shirley has a vivid recollection of that instant. "We had an explosive decompression (cabin pressure fell to zero), the landing gear "unsafe" lights came on, the hydraulic pressures and quantities dropped to zero, our flap gauges went into a frenzy, the cabin altitude horn blared and all the cabin oxygen masks fell out. We were in big trouble!"

A hostess dashed into the cockpit to report a large hole in the right wing above the main landing gear. It seemed that an explosive device had detonated below the cabin floor; the ship

continued to fly more or less normally. "We were down to our standby systems," said Shirley. While First Officer Spence headed back toward Dulles Airport, Shirley went back to assess the situation. "I could see daylight through the wing, the gear was hanging down and there was smoke coming from the well. I told the hostesses to brief the passengers for an emergency landing as I could not be sure what would happen when the wheels contacted the runway."

Second Officer Roger Stephens got busy restoring what power he could with the standby systems. All of the back-up devices for flight control functioned normally. As the crippled jet turned on a long final approach, Stephens manually extended the remaining wheels. All of Dulles' emergency equipment lined the runway, prepared for the worst. The 727 touched down and the damaged right main gear held; crew and passengers were quickly evacuated.

Captain J. R. Shirley, standing in center, with First Officer M. R. Spence (dark tux), Second Officer Roger Stephens and Hostesses (l. to r.) Charlie Kiga, Kristin Rathnow and Francine Urlacker in picture taken at Daedalian awards banquet. The Order of the Daedalians was founded in 1934 to endorse American excellence in air and space activities, to encourage air safety and offer scholarships to young people interested in aviation-related education. Membership includes many famous aviation figures.

Inspection revealed that a dragging right brake had overheated during takeoff and caused its wheel to explode as the flight neared cruising level. Flying metal penetrated the aft cargo bulkhead, releasing cabin pressure. Equipment in the right main wheel well sustained major damage. Wiring and plumbing lines hung down like so much spaghetti. Federal investigators and company officials praised the crew for its professional conduct in coping with the near-disaster. There was also much deserved praise for the stout 727. Said Shirley, "It's just a dynamic airplane . . . fantastic . . . to take the beating it did and still bring us home."

The entire cool-headed crew received the coveted Daedalian Civilian Air Safety Award, given once a year to the airline captain and crew who "have demonstrated the most outstanding ability, judgement and heroism above and beyond normal operational requirements."

In late 1972, a Royal Air Maroc Airlines 727 with King Hassan II aboard was attacked by three jet fighters flown by dissident Moroccan Air Force officers. Machine gun and cannon fire hit the airliner and one fighter rammed its tail, the attack being halted only when the pilot of the royal flight radioed the fighters that the King was dead. The damaged 727 limped into Rabat, Morocco, and the shaken but unharmed monarch stepped off.

King Hassan decorated the 727 itself with the Head of the Order of the Throne, the kingdom's tribute. Boeing sent technicians to repair the damage and the ship returned to scheduled service bearing its well-deserved badge of honor.

The third incident had an unhappy ending. While on a training flight south of its large training center at Oklahoma City, the Federal Aviation Administration's 727 was struck by a small single-engine private plane. The Cessna, with three student pilots hit the Boeing's right horizontal stabilizer, almost knocking it off the aircraft. The small plane fell to earth from 3,000 feet, killing its occupants, but the FAA 727 was skillfully flown back to Will Rogers Airport and landed without further damage.

None of which surprises anyone who remembers how much punishment Boeing's B-17 could absorb and still fly home. They build muscle into airplanes at Seattle.

360 Passengers — 105 Seats

It was an appalling tale from Vietnam that Walter Cronkite related on his CBS Evening News and there was a remarkable bit of film to illustrate the tragedy — soldiers chasing the slow moving airliner along the taxiway, trying to get aboard, scrambling up the rear stairs, into the cargo compartments and wheel wells, finally throwing grenades to stop the plane.

The plane was a World Airways 727-100 sent to Da Nang to help evacuate refugee women and children. Aboard was

"It was a flight into Hell."
— *Captain Healy*

Captain Healy heads back to Saigon with an estimated 360 souls on board his 727. Note damaged left wing, open cargo doors, jammed main wheels and soldier's feet protruding from left wheel well. This remarkable flight was made on March 29, 1975.

World Airways president Edward J. Daly, two reporters and a cameraman. As the plane was loading, word spread that enemy troops were approaching the field. Men of the crack South Vietnamese 1st Division, the Hac Bao (Black Panthers), made a dash for the airliner, shoving women and children aside in their panic. It was immediately apparent that the crowd was out of control so Daly told Capt. Kenneth Healy to take off. As engines were started, soldiers opened fire on the plane; a hand grenade was tossed under the wings in efforts to delay the departure, causing extensive damage to landing gear and flaps. As the plane gathered speed, frantic refugees and soldiers fought each other to get up the stairway with Daly pulling as many as possible aboard.

Healy figures his ship was overloaded by 20,000 pounds. "We estimated there must have been 360 people aboard a ship designed to carry 105. In the cabin there were 268 — this number we know for sure. The baggage compartments were loaded with people and there were attempts to make the flight in the wheel wells and seven did get through that way to Saigon. Witnesses said bodies fell out but I can't say how many. I believe there were 80 to 90 in the lower compartments but an accurate count was not obtained as they unloaded before anyone thought to make a count.

"Some of the problems encountered were an aft stairway that remained partially extended for the entire flight and main wheels which would not retract. Pressurization was impossible so the flight was made at 10,000 feet. Fuel consumption was three times greater than normal and we landed at Saigon with little in the tanks. A grenade explosion removed two-thirds of the left inboard flap. I wholeheartedly praise the abilities of the 727 aircraft. It is a solid, dependable and completely honest aircraft."

Captain Healy is today Vice President of Operations for World Airways.

727 Chronology

June 15, 1954:	Boeing's Model 367-80, the prototype 707, first flew.
October 26, 1958:	Pan American placed the first 707 into service.
December 5, 1960:	Boeing announced a new three-engine jetliner, the 727. United and Eastern each ordered 40.
November 27, 1962:	First 727 rolled out of factory at Renton, Washington.
February 9, 1963:	First flight of the 727.
October 29, 1963:	United took delivery of the first 727 under a provisional FAA certification.
November 3, 1963:	727 completed a 76,000-mile world demonstration tour that included 26 countries.
December 24, 1963:	Formal FAA type-certification.
February 1, 1964:	Eastern initiates first regular 727 commercial service.
May, 1964:	727 completed 14,000-mile United States and Latin America sales trip.
June 10, 1965:	Boeing announced details of the 727QC, a "quick change" cargo version of the 727.
August 5, 1965:	Boeing announced the 727-200 "Stretch". Deliveries set for late 1967.
April 23, 1966:	Northwest Orient placed first 727QC into service.
June 28, 1966:	Air France ordered four 727-200s to be the first European airline to buy the new high-capacity trijet.
June 5, 1967:	Boeing delivered its 1,000th jet airliner, a 707, to American Airlines.
June 29, 1967:	The first 727-200 rolled out.
July 27, 1967:	First flight of the 727-200.
December 11, 1967:	First 727-200 delivered to Northeast Airlines.
December 14, 1967:	Northeast Airlines placed their 727-200 into service.

December 26, 1967:	500th 727 trijet delivered.
April, 1968:	Total 727 orders pass 750 mark.
December 9, 1970:	Boeing announced the 727 Advanced with new engines, improved performance and new interior as standard equipment. Trans Australia and Ansett each order 4.
May 12, 1971:	727 Advanced gross weight increased to 191,000 pounds for take-off.
September 23, 1971:	All Nippon Airways first to order 727 Advanced with higher allowable take-off gross weights. Two are slated for delivery in June 1972.
October, 1971:	Total 727 sales approached 900, including 321 of the -200 "Stretch" models.
March, 1972:	First flight of the 727-200 Advanced.
June, 1972:	All Nippon took delivery of the first 727-200 Advanced.
September, 1972:	Total 727 orders reach 1,000.
November, 1973:	Sterling Airways (Denmark) took delivery of the first 208,000 pound max take-off gross weight 727-200 Advanced.
January, 1974:	Delivery of the 1,000th 727 made to Delta Airlines.
October, 1975:	Autobrakes, auto-spoilers and Mark III anti-skid certified for the 727.
November, 1976:	Automatic Performance Reserve (APR) certificated on 727-200s with JT8D-17R engines.
April, 1977:	727 became the first "standard fuselage" U.S. transport for Category IIIA landing weather minimums (50-foot decision height).
December, 1977:	Worldwide 727 fleet carried its *one billionth* passenger!
January, 1978:	Total 727 orders hit 1,500 as Air Canada announced purchase of 5 additional 727-200s.

727 Operators

Adnan M. Khashoggi

Aerolineas Argentinas

Aero Peru

Air Algerie

Air Asia

Air Canada

Air Charter

Air France

Air Jamaica

Air Mali

Air Malta

Air Micronesia

Air Nauru

Air Panama

Airlift International

Alaska

Alia-Royal Jordanian

Alitalia

Allegheny

All Nippon

ALM-Antilles

American

American Capital

American Flyers

Ansett

Ariana

Northeast

Northwest Orient

Olympic

Pacific

Pacific Southwest

Pacific Western

Pan American

Piedmont

Quebecair

Rockwell International

| Trans Caribbean |
| Trans International |
| Transair Sweden |
| Trans World |
| Tunis Air |
| Turk Hava Yollari |
| United |
| United Technologies |
| Varig |
| Vasp |
| Wardair |
| Western |
| World |
| Yemen |

About the Authors:

Between them, father-and-son Len and Terry Morgan have logged 33,000 hours as captain/copilot/flight engineer in sixteen airliner types including the Boeing 707, 720, 727 and 747. Together they have authored and/or produced thirty-two books plus numerous magazine articles and photographs.

Acknowledgements:

The authors thank all of the companies and individuals who generously cooperated in the production of this book. Specifically, we gratefully acknowledge the invaluable assistance of Gordon S. Williams, John R. Wheeler, Tom Cole, R. L. Loesch, Jr. and S. L. Wallick, Jr. of the Boeing Commercial Airplane Company; Harold Mansfield, author of *Billion Dollar Battle;* John W. R. Taylor, Editor of *Jane's All the World's Aircraft* and Sidney Jackson, Publishing Director of *Jane's Yearbooks;* Captain Kenneth W. Healy, Vice President and Director of Operations — World Airways; Captain Jack Shirley — Braniff International; Second Officers Sandra Simmons and Michael Steen—Braniff International; John A. Cox and Robert E. Weiss of Pratt & Whitney Aircraft; Colonel Robert E. Morris, Editor — *Daedalus Flyer;* Clint Grant, Lou Drendel, Reuben Wagner, and the following airlines and other organizations who provided us with splendid photography: Braniff International, Continental, Air Algerie, Sabena, American, United, Delta, Western, Hapag-Lloyd, Icelandair, Japan Air, Northwest Orient, Ariana Afghan, Korean, Alaska, SAS, Tunis Air, Mexicana, Hughes Airwest, Federal Aviation Agency, Air France, Pan American, TAP, Olympic, Avianca, Condor, TWA, Lufthansa, World, Cruzeiro, Eastern, Garrett Airesearch and United Press International.

The photograph on Page 89 is copyrighted by the Oklahoma Publishing Company and appeared in the *Daily Oklahoman* on July 28, 1973.

The photograph on Page 85 is by Larry Morris of the *Washington Post.*

Reprint from *Jane's All the World's Aircraft 1962/63* courtesy of the Publisher, Macdonald & Jane's, London.